THE ICON
IN THE LIFE OF THE
CHURCH

INSTITUTE OF RELIGIOUS ICONOGRAPHY
STATE UNIVERSITY GRONINGEN

ICONOGRAPHY OF RELIGIONS

EDITED BY

Th. P. van Baaren, L. P. van den Bosch, L. Leertouwer, F. Leemhuis
and H. Buning (*Secretary*)

SECTION XXIV: CHRISTIANITY

FASCICLE EIGHT

LEIDEN
E. J. BRILL
1981

THE ICON
IN THE LIFE OF THE CHURCH

DOCTRINE · LITURGY · DEVOTION

BY

GEORGE GALAVARIS

With 48 Plates

LEIDEN
E. J. BRILL
1981

ISBN   90 04 06402 8

To

Olympia Galavaris, my mother
Kurt and Josepha Weitzmann, my mentors

CONTENTS

FOREWORD

This study attempts to suggest ways of approaching the 'iconography' of the icon and within set limits to contribute to the statement by the Editors of the Series that "Image, words and actions are not contrasted, the use of one emerges into the use of another." This is particularly true for the icon which cannot be separated from the doctrine, the liturgy and popular devotion. In fact this difficulty is inherent in the Easten Church which has always tried to avoid any separation between theology and mysticism, between liturgy and personal devotion. Although a distinction of topics and corresponding grouping of pictures have been attempted, we hope the text shows that such distinctions do not exist in reality and that in the main it must be left to the reader to re-unite what here is put asunder. The icon must be envisaged as a whole

According to this concept we have not always followed traditional classifications. For example, not all icons of Christ are grouped together. Some of them have strong liturgical connotations and deserve to be included in a section dealing with the Icon and Worship. In our order of presentation priority was given to the Mother of God over the angels because from the theological point of view, the angels bear the image of God in them but lack the body given to man who can participate in the earthly life. Man has been granted the image of God in greater fullness. Furthermore we considered it important to draw attention to icons which reflect the ritual and demonstrate the significance of the cult of icons and of relics for the believer. The inclusion of icons devoted to the cult of Mary needs no explanation, for Mariolatry takes indeed a high place in the East as it does in the West.

In a work like this, I have relied heavily on learned studies, cited in the bibliography. I would like, however, to single out the work of Gerardus van der Leeuw, *Vom Heiligen in der Kunst*, translated into English as *Sacred and Profane Beauty*, London 1963. It is a singularly stimulating, seminal book.

This study could not have been accomplished without the photos and the necessary permission for publication. Museums and private collectors have assisted the project eagerly. All photos, unless otherwise stated have been provided by them. I kindly ask them to find here my personal expression of gratitude. My debt to Professor Kurt Weitzmann for his many kindnesses I am not permitted to mention.

G.G.

ACKNOWLEDGMENTS

The author and publisher would like to express their sincere thanks to the following institutions and individuals who kindly provided photographs and granted permission to reproduce them in this book.

Aachen, Suermondt-Ludwig-Museum, pl. XLVIa (Photo, Anne Gold, Casino Str. 29); Pfarrer W. Zimmermann and the Abtei Church St. Johan-Bart., pl. XXIIIc (Photo, Dr. H-M. Franke, Grashofweg Str., Ratingen)

Amsterdam, Mr M. van Rijn, V.O.F. Art Trade, pls. IIb, IVc, XXIIa, XXVIIIc

Athens, Dr. M. Chatzidakis, pls. XVa, XXIc, XXIIb; Dr. A. Delivorrias, Director, and the Benaki Museum, pls. IVa, Vb, XVIc, XXVb, and from the Photographic Archives of the same Museum pls. XIIc, XIXc, XXIb, XXIIIb (Photos, Papachatzidakis); Mr. P. Lazarides, Director, the Byzantine Museum and the T.A.P.A. Service, 17 Philellinon St. pls. VIII, IXc, XVIa, XXVIIa, XXXb, XXXVIIa, XXXVIIIc; Mrs. J. Vassiliadis and the Lomberdo Museum, pl. XXIVa; Dr. D. Papastamos, Director, and the National Gallery of Greece-Museum A. Soutzos, pls. Xc, XVIb

Athos, Archimandrite Basil, Prior, and the Monastery of Stavroniketa, pl. XVIIb (Photo, National Bank of Greece)

Belgrade, Dr. V. Kondiĉ, Director, and the National Museum, pls. XVb, XXVIIIb; Dr. G. Suboticĉ, Director, and the Museum of Applied Arts, pl. XXVa

Berlin, W., Profs. Drs. P. Bloch, V. H. Elbern and the Skulpturengallerie-Frühchristlich-Byzantinischer Sammlung, Staatliche Museen Preussischer Kulturbesitz, pl. XIXa (Photo, Jörg P. Anders, W. Berlin)

Cleveland, Miss D.G. Shepherd and the Cleveland Museum of Art (Purchase, Leonard C. Hanna Jr. Bequest Fund), pl. VIIb

Cyprus, Dr. V. Karagiorgis, Director of Antiquities, and the Cyprus Museum, Nicosia, pls. XXIa, XXIIc, XLVIc, XLVIIa

Echteld, Nederland, Mr. R. Roozemond, Director, and the Icon Centre, Kasteel "De Wijenburgh", pls. VIc, IXb, XIIIb, XIXb, XXc, XXVIb, XXVIIc

Freising, Dr. P. Steiner, Director, and the Diözesan Museum, pl. VIIa

Geneva, Miss J. Doebelli and the Musée d'Art et d'Histoire, pl. XLIIIa

Houston, Texas, The Museum of Fine Arts (Gift of Miss Annete Finnigan), pl. XIb

Kölliken, Switzerland, Dr. Med. Dent. S. Amberg-Herzog (Collection open to the public), pls. XXIXb, XLa and b

London, The Temple Gallery, pl. IVb

Madison, Wisconsin, The Director and the Elvehjem Museum of Art, The University of Wisconsin, pls. XI, XXIXc

Moscow, The Tretyakov Gallery, pls. Ic, IIIb, Vc, XIIb, XXa, XXXII, XLIa, XLVIb; and pl. XXXIIIb and c (Photos, Bildarchiv Foto Marburg)

Munich, Stadtmuseum, pl. XLIIb

Ottawa, Dr. Myron Laskin Jr. and the National Gallery of Canada, (Bequest of Frederick Hudd, Compton, Surrey, England 1969), pl. XXVIIb

Oxford, The Ashmolean Museum, Dept. Western Art, pl. XVc

Palermo, Soprintendenza alle Gallerie ed opere d'arte della Sicilia, pl. Va

Paris, Dr. Ch. Desroches Noblecourt, Conservateur en Chef, et le Départment des Antiquités égyptiennes du Musée du Louvre, pl. XXVIIIa

Patmos, Archimandrite Isidoros, Prior, and the Monastery of St. John the Theologian, pls. XXIIIa, XXXIVa, XLVIII (Photos, National Bank of Greece)

Princeton, N. J., The Art Museum, Princeton University (Gift of Prof. Allan Marquand), pl. VIa; Professor K. Weitzmann for his eagerness to help with the material from Sinai

Recklinghausen, Dr. H. Skrobucha, Kustos, and the Ikonen-Museum, pls. XXXIVc, XXXVIIIb

Rhode Island, U.S.A., Miss R. Sandgren and the Museum of Art, Rhode Island School of Design (Museum appropriation), pl. XXXVc

Richenthal-Luzern, Switzerland, Pfarrer J.K. Felber, pls. IIIc, XLIV

Rome, S. Croce in Gerusaleme, Gabinetto photographico nazionale, pl. XXXVa

Sewickley, PA., The late R.H. Hann, pls. XVIIa, XXVc

Sinai, Monastery of St Catherine, pls. Ia, IIIa, IXa, Xa, XIIa, XIIIa, XIV, XXVIa, XXXa, XXXIa, XXXVb, XXXIXa, XLVIIb (published through the courtesy of the Michigan-Princeton-Alexandria Expedition to Mount Sinai)

Stockholm, Miss E. Karlsson and the National Museum, pl. Ib

Toronto, Mr. L. Cselenyi and the Royal Ontario Museum, pls. XXVIc, XXXVIa, XLIIa

Venice, O. Böhm, pl. VIb; Prof. Dr. M. Manoussacas, Director and the Hellenic Institute, pls. IIa, XVIII, XXXIIIa reprinted from the publications of the Institute cited in the commentary on the plates

Vienna, Prof. Dr. G. Egger, Mr. C. Nödland the Österreichisches Museum für Angewandte Kunst, pl. XXXVIIb; The Director and the Kunsthistorisches Museum, pls.XXb, XXXVIIIa, XLV

Zumikon, Switzerland, Dr. Ing. Hans Bibus, pls. XXIXa, XXXIXb

BIBLIOGRAPHY

This bibliography does not claim to be complete; only the more important works or those where illustrations and bibliographies are to be found are cited.

ALPATOV, M. V., *Altrussische Ikonenmalerei*, Dresden 1958.
——, *Colour in Early Russian Icon Painting*, Russian and English, Moscow 1974.
ANTONOVA, M. N., and MNEVA, N. E., *Gosudarstvennaia Tret'iakovskaia gallereia. Katalog drevnerusskoi zhivopisi XI-nachala XVIII V.V.*, 2 vols., Moscow 1963.
ANTONOVA, V., *Drevnerusskoe iskusstvo sobranii Pavla Korina*, Moscow 1966.
BALABANOV, K., *Icons of Macedonia*, Skopje 1969.
BANCK, A., *Byzantine Art in the Collections of the USSR*, Leningrad-Moscow 1969.
BERTELLI, C., "The 'Image of Pity' in Santa Croce in Gerusaleme," *Essays in the History of Art, Presented to Rudolf Wittkower*, London 1967, 40-55.
BOLSHAKOVA, L., and KMENSKAYA, E., *State Tretyakov Gallery-Early Russian Art*, Moscow 1968.
CHATZIDAKIS, M., "Ho zographos Euphrosynos," *Kretika Chronika*, 10 (1956), 273-291.
——, *Icônes de Saint-Georges des Grecs et de la Collection de l'institut Hellénique de Venise*, Venice 1962 and *Eikones*, Album, Venice 1975.
——, "Icônes d'architraves provenant du Mont Athos," *Deltion Christianikes Archaeologikes Hetaireias*, per. 4, 4 (1964), Athens 1966, 377-403.
——, *Eikones tes Patmou*, Athens 1977.
CHATZIDAKIS M., et al., *Les icônes dans les collections suisses*, Berne 1968.
DANILOWA, I. J., *Dionissi*, Vienna-Munich 1970.
DJURIĆ, V. J. D., *Icônes de Yugoslavie*, Belgrade 1961.
DOBSCHUTZ, G., *Christusbilder*, Leipzig 1899.
DOGNANOVIĆ, D., DJURIĆ, V. J., MEDOKOVIĆ, D., *Chilandar on the Holy Mountain*, Belgrade 1978.
EGGER, G., *Späte griechische Ikonen*, Vienna 1970.
ELBERN, V. H. *Ikonen aus der frühchristlich-byzantinischer Sammlung, Staatliche Museen preussischer Kulturbesitz-Berlin*, Berlin 1970.
EMBIRICOS, A., *L'école crétoise, dernière phase de la peinture byzantine*, Paris 1967.
EVDOKIMOV, P., *L'art de l'icône; théologie de la beauté*, Paris 1970.
FELICETTI-LIEBENFELS, W., *Geschichte der byzantinischen Ikonenmalerei*, Olten-Lausanne 1956.
—— *Geschichte der russischen Ikonenmalerei*, Graz 1972.
GALAVARIS, G., "The Stars of the Virgin: an Ekphrasis of an Icon of the Mother of God," *Eastern Churches Review*, 1(1967, 1968), 364-369.
——, *Icons from the Elvehjem Center*, The University of Wisconsin, Madison 1973.
——, "Christ with Saints Alexandra and Agatha. A Russian Icon in the National Gallery of Canada," *Bulletin, The National Gallery of Canada*, 26 (1975), 24-38.
——, "A Bread Stamp from Sinai and its Relatives," *Jahrbuch der österreichischen Byzantinistik*, 27 (1978), 329-342.
——, "The Portraits of St. Athanasius of Athos," *Byzantine Studies/Etudes Byzantines*, 5(1978), 96-124.
——, "Majestas Mariae. The Glorification of the Mother of God in Greek and Russian Icons," *Icons and East Christian Works of Art*, M. van Rijn ed., Amsterdam 1980, 7-18.
GERHARD, H. P., *Welt der Ikonen*, 3rd ed., Recklinghausen 1970.
GOUMA-PETERSON, T., "The Dating of Creto-Venetian Icons: A reconsideration in Light of New Evidence," *Allen Memorial Art Museum Bulletin*, 30 (1972), 12-21.
GRABAR, A., *L'iconoclasme byzantin. Dossier archéologique*, Paris 1957.
—— *La Sainte Face de Laon*, Prague 1931.
——, *Les revêtements en or et en argent des icones byzantines du moyen âge*, Venice 1975.
HENDRIKS, P., *Ikonen*, Amsterdam 1960.
IRIMIE, C., FOCSA, M., *Romanian Icons Painted on Glass*, Bucharest 1968.
KJELLIN, H., *Rysska ikoner i svensk och norsk ägo*, Stockholm 1956.
KLOSINSKA, J., *Ikonenmuseum Recklinghausen, Ikonen aus Polen*, Exhibition Catalogue, Recklinghausen 1966

KONDAKOV, N. P., *Russkaia Ikona*, 4 vols, Prague 1928-29, 1931, 1933.
KONSTANTINOWICZ, J. B., *Ikonostasis. Studien und Forschungen*, Lwov 1939.
KREIDL-PAPADOPOULOS, K., "Die Ikonen im Kunsthistorischen Museum in Wien," *Jarhbuch der Kunsthistorischen Sammlungen in Wien*, 66, n.S. 30 (1970), 49-134.
Kunst der Ostkirche, Stift Herzogenburg, Exhibition Catalogue, Vienna 1977.
LANGE, R., *Die byzantinische Reliefikone*, Recklinghausen 1964.
LAZAREV, V. N., *Andrej Rublev i evo shkola*, Moscow 1966.
——— *Theophanes der grieche und sein Schule*, Vienna-Munich 1968.
———, *Moscovskaia shkola ikonopisi*, Russian and English, Moscow 1971, in German, Berlin 1977.
MASLENITSYN, S. I., *Isaroslavskaia ikonopis'* (Album), Russian and English, Moscow 1973.
ONASCH, K., *Ikonen*, Gütersloh 1961 (also in French and English, Paris, London 1961).
OUSPENSKY, L., *Essai sur la théologie de l'icone dans l'Eglise Orthodoxe*, 1, Paris 1960, also in English, Crestwood, N. York 1978.
———, "Vopros ikonostasa" in *Message de l'Exarchat du Patriarche russe en Europe occidentale* 44 (1963), 223-252.
OUSPENSKY, L., LOSSKY, V., *The Meaning of Icons* Boston, 1952.
OUCHINNIKOV, A. N., *Zhivopis drevnego Pskova XIII-CIV veka*, Moscow 1971.
PALLAS, D., "He Theotokos rothon to amaranton," *Archaeologikon Deltion*, 26 (1972), 225[ff].
PAPAGEORGIOU, A., *Ikonen aus Zypern*, Munich-Geneva-Paris-London 1969.
RADOJČIĆ, S., *Icônes de Serbie et de Macedoine*, Belgrade 1961.
TALBOT RICE, TAMARA, *Russian Icons*, London 1963.
TALBOT RICE, DAVID and TAMARA, *Icons and Their Dating*, London 1974.
TALBOT RICE, D., et al., *The Icons of Cyprus*, London 1937.
RIZZI, A., "Le icone bizantine e postbizantine delle chiese veneziane," *Thesauresmata*, 9 (1972), pp. 250-291.
ROOZEMOND VAN GINHOVEN, HETTY, J., *Ikon, Kunst-Geist und Glaube*, Exhibition Catalogue, Recklinghausen and Echteld 1980.
ROTHEMUND, B., *Handbuch der Ikonenkunst*, 2nd ed., Munich 1966.
ROTHEMUND et al., *Katalog des Ikonenmuseums Schloss Autenried*, Munich 1974.
SCHILLER, G., *Ikonographie der christlichen Kunst*, 2 vols., Gütersloh 1966 also in English, London 1971.
SKROBUCHA, H., *Von Geist und Gestalt der Ikonen*, Recklinghausen 1961, also in English, N. York 1965.
———, *Kunstsammlungen der Stadt Recklinghausen, Ikonen-Museum*, Catalogue, 4th ed., Recklinghausen 1968.
———, *Ikonen, Haus der Kunst München*, Exhibition Catalogue, Munich 1969.
SOTIRIOU, G., "Eikon ethimon tes mones Sinai kai historikon skenon tes erimou," *Deltion christianikes archaeologikes hetaireias*, per. 4, 2 (1960-1961), Athens 1962, 1[ff].
SOTIRIOU, GEORGES and MARIA, *Icones du Mont Sinai*, 1 (Plates), 2 (Text), Athens 1956, 1958, in Greek with French summary.
STUART, J., *Ikons*, London 1975.
TATIĆ-DJURIČ, M., "Le Baptême de Jesus-Christ icone datant de l'époque de la Renaissance des Paléologues," *Recueil du Musée National, Belgrade* 4(1964), 267-281.
———, "L'icône de la Vierge Peribleptos son origine et sa diffusion," in *Festschrift S. Radojčić*, Belgrade 1969, 335-354.
———, "L'icône de la Vierge du Signe," *Sbornik sa likovne umetnosti*, 13, Novi Sad, 1977, 1-26.
TRUBETSKOI, E. N., *Icons: Theology in Colour*, (trans. from the Russian), N. York 1973.
VELTHUIS, B., *De Zoon, Christus op Ikonen*, Echteld-Nederland 1980.
VELTHUIS, B., ROOZEMOND, R., GERRITSEN-SAWWIK, V., *Ikon-Maria*, Echteld-Nederland 1979.
WALTER, CH., "Les origines de l'iconostase," *Eastern Churches Review*, 3 (1971), 251-267.
WEITZMANN, K., "The Mandylion and Constantine Porphyrogennetos," *Cahiers archéologiques*, 11 (1960), 163-184.
———, "Fragments of an Early St. Nicholas Triptych on Mt. Sinai," *Deltion christianikes archaeologikes hetaireias*, per. 4, 4 (1964), Athens 1966, 1-23.
——— "Icon Painting in the Crusader Kingdom," *Dumbarton Oaks Papers*, 20 (1966), 50-83.
———, "Byzantine Miniature and Icon Painting in the Eleventh Century," *Proceedings of the XIIIth Inter. Congress of Byzantine Studies, Oxford 1966*, London 1967, 209-224.
———, "The Cycle of the Great Feasts," NEW GRECIAN GALLERY, *Feast Day Icons*, Exhibition Catalogue London 1973, no pagination.
———, *The Monastery of Saint Catherine at Mount Sinai. The Icons*, 1. From the Sixth to the Tenth Century, Princeton 1976.
———, *The Icon*, N. York 1978.

WEITZMANN, K., CHATZIDAKIS, M., MIATEV, K., RADOJčIć, S., *Frühe Ikonen*, Vienna-Munich 1965 and
    several editions in English, French, Russian, Dutch, Spanish, Italian and Yugoslav.
WEITZMANN, K., CHATZIDAKIS, M,. RADOJčIć, S., *Die Ikonen*, Sinai, Griechenland und Yugoslawien,
    Herrsching-Ammersee 1977.
WENDT, C. H., *Rumänische Ikonenmalerei*, Eisenach 1953.
XYNGOPOULOS, A., *Katalogos ton eikonon, Mouseiou Benaki*, Athens 1936.
——, *Schediasma tes threskeutikes zographikes meta ten alosin*, Athens 1957.

INTRODUCTION

Icons, East and West

Christianity yielded to the power of representation early enough, despite the hesitation or even the opposition of certain early writers. Among various symbols and a choice of episodes from the Old and New Testaments which the Christians set on the walls of the baptisteries and tombs, a special place was given to portraits of donors, benefactors, dignitaries of the Church or State, Christ, martyrs, saints.

In portraying these persons, Christians continued an established tradition which had reached its peak in Hellenistic and Roman times.[1] Statues of emperors, officials, dramatists, writers adorned market places, libraries, portrait of emperors were carried in processions as part of the imperial cult and wealthy citizens took pride in possessing portraits of their ancestors. It seems, however, that essential contributions to the formation of the Christian portrait were made by the imperial portrait, by portraits in bust form included in a shield—known as the *imago clipeata*, common on sarcophagi already since the third century, the consul's portrait made on an ivory diptych, and the Egyptian mummy portraits of which most famous have been those discovered at Fayum. The relationship between the Fayum and Christian portraits can be seen on panels painted in Coptic Egypt which are remarkable for their frozen, stiff design and strong expressiveness (Pl. XXVIIIa).

These images (the Greek word is *eikon*) were self-contained paintings on wood but when they were set in churches they were copied on the walls in fresco and eventually in mosaic depending on their devotional purposes. As the Church grew and the use of the holy portraits—the icons—responding to a popuplar demand, was disseminated throughout the Christian world, materials such as ivory, mosaic, stone, silver, enamel, wood, bone and even mother of pearl were used and various shapes were adopted of which most popular became the rectangle and forms associated with it. The technique was also changed and the portraits were painted in tempera with egg as binding medium.

However, it should be stressed that the Christian portraits were set apart from the glorious Greco-Roman creations by the message conveyed by their wide-opened eyes. Whereas the statues of emperors had a majesty and expressed Otherness in a contrived look, the portraits of saints had the expression of inner peace. The respect the Christians felt for the heroes of their faith prompted them to honour their portraits following general practices pertaining to the cult of the emperor and veneration of officials. Candles were lit beside the icons, veils hung over them and flowers were offered to them. Whereas in the first centuries of Christianity people venerated and worshiped the graves of the martyrs and their relics, they later came to venerate their images and at last to worship their icons, that is to say images which were not common portraits, representing a person in the corruptible state of his flesh, but images showing man partaking of divine life.

---

[1] Weitzmann, K., *The Icon*, N. York 1978, pp. 7ff; Galavaris, G., *Icons from the Elvehjem Art Center*, The University of Wisconsin, Madison 1973, pp. 1ff.

Because of the need of a personal communion between the supplicant and the sanctified man, the authenticity of the image was of great importance. If an authentic image was not possible, a definite 'type' of a particular person was created which could not be changed. Its creation was the work of the Church and belonged to Tradition. Often to secure the authenticity of the image, legends were created about icons not made by human hands— the *acheropoietoi*—most important of which was the Edessa image of Christ (Pl. III). These legends were also used in support of the images in the eighth and ninth centuries, when the opposition against the icon shook the foundations of the Byzantine empire and had important repercussions in the West, taking the form of a civil war, the *iconoclastic controversy*. The iconophiles used these legends and argued that the countenance of Christ on his own icon was an epiphany, because the first icon ever to come into existence was made miraculously. This is why an icon can perform miracles, listen to prayers and provide answers.[2]

Icons did not only contain holy portraits. It was natural for the great events of the Church, —the histories— whether the life of Christ or of the Saints, which had already adorned religious buildings and holy books, to find a place in icons. Eventually an interchange of themes between icons and other media is to be observed, due to the fact that all the arts form part of the liturgy, each contributing to the sacramental life of the believer.

Although icons appeared everywhere, it was in Constantinople that their particular language was developed and their doctrine was formulated. In the Council Quinisexte (September, 692) the icon was related to the doctrine of the Incarnation. The Word became flesh, dwelt among us, and therefore an image must represent that which was revealed to man. The reflection of the divine glory in the icon was possible. The conclusions of this Council were not unanimously accepted by the Church of Rome. It was difficult for the Western mind to understand the philosophical complexities of the Greeks. Nevertheless, during the iconoclastic controversy which ended with the triumph of the iconophiles and the restoration of the images in 843, the Latin West supported the decisions of the Greek Church. That is, it supported the icons, the cult of the saints and their relics. But the effects of this crisis were different in each area. Generally speaking, in the West it was the cult of relics that was developed more.[3] In the East, the icon achieved its final theological formulation and its integration in the liturgy.

Between the Latin and Greek theologians there was a different understanding of the meaning and purpose of the icon. For the West a representation of a holy person or event remained a means of instruction, although the West knew also the wonder-working icon. The differences are summed up in the *Libri Carolini* where it is stated that the Greeks place all their hope on the icons whereas the Latins venerate the saints in their relics or even in their vestments.[4] A different mind is at work. One, the Western is more concrete, prefers to express itself in stone rather than in painting. The other, the Greek, philosophical and abstract, led to a metaphysical interpretation of the icon which explains the vital role the icon played in the Eastern Church. In the West the artist was left free to interpret the religious episodes according to his own concepts and emotions. And, although

---

[2] Meer van der F., *Early Christian Art*, London 1967, pp. 104, 105[f].
[3] Ouspensky, L., *Essai sur la théologie de l'icone dans l'Eglise Orthodoxe*, i, Paris 1960, pp. 110[ff]. *Ibid.*, p. 140.
[4] L.2, Ch. XXVI; Ouspensky, *op. cit.*, p. 169.

sculptures, mostly of the Mother of God and saints, often became objects of liturgical cult, the icon as such, remained unknown to the West. Religious panels in churches were not considered revelations of a metaphysical reality. Even in Italy where for centuries Byzantine art was greatly venerated and religious panels were produced much like Byzantine icons, sometimes copying them, these remained religious paintings only. They lacked the confrontation of man with the Holy. Since the Gothic period, the West was interested in presenting the state of one's emotions when one attempted to raise himself towards God. In the East, through the icon, the grace of a personal meeting with the Divine was bestowed upon the faithful. The icon made the Holy present. The religious panel expressed what man felt about the Holy.

The icon was developed and established in Byzantium which, after its fall, continued to be the source of spiritual life for the entire Orthodox Church. In the hands of the Greeks, the direct heirs of Byzantium, icon painting continued in the monasteries of the mainland, in the islands, and above all in Crete whose painters through contacts with the West, especially with Venice, enriched the repertory of iconography in the sixteenth and seventheenth century.

The spirit of Byzantium was transmitted to the Slavic world and it continued to be expressed in profound works of Russian theologians stemming from the writings of the Greek Fathers; by the presence of Greek artists and through the dissemination of Greek icons. One of the most venerated icons in Russia, the Virgin of Vladimir, was brought from Constantinople in the twelfth century and became the source of inspiration for generations of iconographers. It is not an exaggeration to say that up to the days of the great Rublyov the Russians remained faithful to what they learned from the Greeks. But they added to this another dimension of mysticism responding to special needs of the Slavic soul, which was made visible in the icon by a new treatment of form: a visionary abstraction and fiery colours.

The Meaning of the Icon

The *kontakion* sung at the festival of the restoration of the images, Sunday of Orthodoxy, gives us the entire significance of the Icon.[5] Christ, by imbuing human nature with Divine life and Divine beauty made possible the redemption of matter. Matter can become spirit. Once man accepts the meaning of the Incarnation, a new way of life is open to him. This is why the icon is linked with the main themes that dominate Christian life: Incarnation, life-in-Christ, man's deification.

Based on Neo-Platonic theories, the icon is thought basically a mystery, a vehicle of divine power and grace, a means of God's knowledge. It is not merely a symbol of the archetype, but the represented becomes present through the icon. The Council of Nicea of 787 declared that at the adoration of the icon of Christ the faithful should say, "this is Christ the Son of God." This concept is echoed throughout the centuries. In a Russian work, to bring a recent example only, written anonymously in the nineteenth century, entitled *The Way of a Pilgrim*, which deals with the meaning of inner prayer, the following episode is narrated. The pilgrim is offered hospitality, and entering the study of his host describes what he sees as follows: "what a lot of books there were and beautiful icons, and

---

[5] For the Greek text see, *Triodion*, Athens 1960, p. 137.

the life-giving Cross with the Figure life-sized and the Gospels lying near it. I said a prayer and then to my host 'You are in God's own Paradise', I said. 'Here is the Lord Jesus Christ himself and his most Holy Mother and the Blessed Saints'...'' [6]

The icon participates in the holiness of the represented. Through the icon the beholder becomes a participant of divine life, a concept based on the doctrine of the image of God which was put into man at the time of Creation. For man was made in the image and likeness of God (Gen. I: 26, 27; V: 1) which has been interpreted by the Fathers as man, created by God in the image of God, is called upon to acquire the Divine likeness and fulfill the final purpose of the Creation, its deification.[7] Therefore, there is a relation between the icon and the image of God which man carries within himself, the concept of the image becoming the central point in the process of creation. For in the last analysis, images of the image of God participate in its divine character. These ideas are current in Christian thought as, for example, one sees in the meditations of the Russian archpriest John Sergieff of St. Andrew's cathedral at Gronstadt, Russia (d. 1908) recorded in his diary.[8]

The theme of the transfiguration of nature and man's deification—man becomes god by grace—is declared in the Eastern Church through the liturgical arts. The icon is one of them and in its own way it reveals the incorruptible kingdom of God. The prototype, represented by material means, belongs to the corrupt world. Its transcedental quality, however, can be expressed by the fixation of the type which removes that which is represented from all that is ephemeral. The icons are then "pure fixation." [9] This is why icons cannot be painted according to the imagination of the artists or a living model. The relationship between the prototype and the image would have been lost. For this reason the icon-painter uses manuals, like the Greek *Hermeneia* or the Russian *Podlinnik*, which describe the iconographic scenes and colours to be used. But the use of manuals alone does not guarantee the painting of the sacred image. The painter must himself be "illuminated." This is why, according to tradition, St. Luke painted the icon of the Virgin after the Pentecost.

The predominant feature ascribed to saints by the Church is light. If the icon is to make this visible, it must have its own language. Forms and colours must show the metaphysical luminosity of the represented, they must manifest what the eye has not seen but without suppressing all that is human. For this purpose everything is represented in its relation to the Divine. Naturalism is put aside and men and landscapes are shown in a transfigured state. Van der Leeuw expresses this thought beautifully, saying: "but whoever expects a luxuriance of beautiful form in the art of the icons will be disappointed. The divine has a form, but it is the broken form of Christ; it is an image which is bearable only when a person renounces all outward beauty, all luxury of form." [10] This is the divine "reality" experienced by Eastern ascetics in their own lives exemplified in the following extract from the *Pratum spirituale* by John Moschus (seventh century), chapter CIV: "...and another one of the old men of the same *coenobium* told this about Abbâ Nonnus, saying,

[6] French, R. M., Trans., *The Way of a Pilgrim*, London 1954, pp. 82[ff].

[7] Lossky, V. N., *The Mystical Theology of the Eastern Church*, London 1957.

[8] Goulaeff, E. E., Trans., *My Life in Christ* (Extracts from the Diary of the Archpriest John Sergieff), London 1897, esp. pp. 488, 489.

[9] Leeuw van der G., *Sacred and Profane Beauty*, London 1963, p. 175.

[10] *Ibid.*, p. 175.

'One night before the nocturnal *semantron* was heard leaving my cell I made for the church and I saw the old man standing in front of the church and praying having his hands stretched towards the sky. And his hands were shown as if they were torches of fire. And seized by fear, I left.'" [11]

ICONS AND WORSHIP

The icon is an indispensable part of the liturgy which in its turn functions as an "icon" revealing the divine presence to the faithful and uniting the celestial and terrestrial Church. The contact, however, between the faithful and the world of grace is established through the icon, for it is the icon the believer confronts and with which he converses. And this is the icon's first and foremost liturgical function. Broadly speaking, this is accomplished by the role played by the icon in the actual ritual, that is in the performance of the liturgy, and by the pictorialization of the message of the liturgy.[12]

In the Eastern Church an image becomes an icon through a special ceremony of consecration which varies from a simple benediction to anointing the holy image with myrrh.[13] The consecrated icon finds a place in the church, on the walls, on special icon shrines, on the ambo, on the chandeliers (this is true mostly in monastic churches—these icons are bilateral and of small size), on the *proskynetarion*, a pulpit-like stand within the church. Here one normally sees the day's icon, that is the one representing or related to the festival of the day. Icons form also the *iconostasis*, the screen separating the chancel from the sanctuary, which has three doors. The central one (the royal doors) leads to the altar, the one to the left opens to the prothesis and that to the right to the diaconicon. In Byzantium the iconostasis was formed of two rows of icons. On the lower range there were the large, almost life-size icons of Christ, Mary, the titular saint of the church and the archangel Michael. On the upper register there was an extended *Deesis* and icons of the Great Feasts of the Church.

In the Slavic lands, particularly in Russia, the iconostasis, made of carved wood, became very high with five rows of icons: the first row, as in Byzantium contained the titular saint, among other icons, the second row formed an extended Deesis called *čin*. The Church Feasts constituted the third range and that above them contained the prophets (fourth row) placed on either side of the Virgin of the Sign (*Žnamenje*), while the patriarchs and forefathers formed the last row. The iconostasis doors are also made of icons. The royal doors—often but not always—contain icons of the four Evangelists, the Annunciation and the Communion of the Apostles ((Pl. XXXII). The side doors can have icons of the archangels Michael and Gabriel or of the first deacons Stephen and Philip or even the writers of the two principal liturgies, John Chrysostom and Basil the Great. The development of the iconostasis resulted in a complicated symbolism, the problems of which will be introduced below.

When the Orthodox enters the church he offers a candle to the icon on the proskynetarion, kisses it, proceeds to the wonder-working icon, if the church has one, and to the lower icons of the iconostasis, where one finds the most ancient and often miraculous icons.

---

[11] Migne, *PG*, 87, III, 2961.

[12] Suttner, E. Ch., "Ikonen und Kult," in *Kunst der Ostkirche*, Stift Herzogenburg, Exhibition Catalogue, Vienna 1977, pp. 45-51.

[13] Rothemund, B. *Handburch der Ikonenkunst*, 2nd ed., Munich 1966, pp. 340, 341.

Having venerated them, the faithful would contemplate the upper icons which display Christ's redemptive work.

The iconostasis plays an important part in the liturgy. The priest and the deacon recite prayers and cense the icons, especially those left and right of the royal doors, making the presence and participation of the Holy Person real, so that as the liturgy develops, the function and symbolism of the iconostasis becomes clear.

At the beginning of the preparation of the priest for the liturgy, the priest bows before the icons of the iconostasis and the icon placed on the proskynetarion and standing before the iconostasis he invokes "the Heavenly King, the Paraclete," to "come and abide in us...", subsequently he says three prayers before the icons of the Saviour, his Mother, and St. John the Baptist, and he kisses these and the other icons on the iconostasis. The prayer to Christ opens with the following words, "thy most pure icon we venerate oh gracious One...," while that to Mary begins with the words "Thou who art the source of mercy..." The prayers end with the following prayer "Lord, stretch forth Thy hand..." which is one of the most significant and oldest of all preparatory prayers in the *Proskomide*. The contents of these prayers, addressed to the icons, express the sentiments of the priest before he enters the altar. On behalf of the congregation he begs for forgiveness and expresses his confidence in God's mercy for man who is the work of His hands. Another source of mercy, "Source of Life", is the Mother of God.[14]

At the beginning of the Liturgy of the Catechumens, the iconostasis-icons receive censing by the deacon or by the priest and so do the participants in the liturgy. The act of censing expresses reverence but it is also a symbolic sign of the *presence* of those represented on the icons. Censing the icons is also prescribed just before the Great Entrance begins (the solemn procession transferring the gifts from the Prothesis to the altar), and the prayers recited on this occasion have a similarity to the introductory prayers.[15] Finally at the conclusion of the liturgy, before the so-called prayer *Behind the Ambo*, the priest addresses once more the icon of Christ Pantocrator and the faithful kiss the icons before they depart. But icons do not relate to the liturgy through the ritual only.

The rite of the Prothesis (the Preparation of the Eucharistic Gifts) involves the arrangement of the particles of the Eucharistic bread on the patten, which symbolizes the unity of the Church, comprising the living saints on earth and those who triumphed in Heaven, around the Sacrificial Lamb.[16] This symbolism is reflected on the general programme of the iconostasis. In a more particular way the icon of the Deesis, and those above the čin pictorialize the intercession prayer of the Church recited in the Epiclesis (prayer invoking the descent of the Holy Spirit) at the Holy Anaphora (the words of institution of the Sacrament). However the heart of the liturgy is the Holy Eucharist. Before the consecration of the species takes place, the priest recites silently the Eucharistic prayer containing the very words of Christ used in the institution of the Sacrament. The priest pronounces the words of consecration in the first person, as if he were Christ, the High Priest. For the priest is, according to St. Maximus, "the icon of God himself." [17] What follows, including the consumption of the Eucharistic sacrifice makes it clear that the Eucharist

[14] Solovey, M. M., *The Byzantine Divine Liturgy*, Washington, D.C. 1970, pp. 112-114.
[15] *Ibid.*, pp. 142, 223, 225.
[16] Galavaris, G., *Bread and the Liturgy*, Madison-Milwakee-London 1970, pp. 62[f], 181[ff].
[17] Commentaries of Maximus the Confessor to the works of Pseudo-Dionysius, Migne, *PG*, 4, 140.

"is a celebration which gives a glimpse to the whole humanity of the Kingdom of Heaven" and brings the faithful in unity with Christ.[18]

This symbolism is embodied in the iconostasis which in the Words of Symeon of Thessalonica (d. 1429) is the image of the Church's unity in Christ. Later, this symbolism is amplified in Russian writings and the iconostasis expresses the union in love of all creatures with their creator—*sobornost*; it manifests a transfigured world and the eternal presence of Christ (Mt. 28:20).[19]

There are, however, two iconostasis-icons which make clear the role of the priest at the consecration and the communion. One icon, known after the fall of Constantinople, shows Christ as the High Priest (sometimes this icon is placed on the throne of the bishop) (Pl. XI). The other icon represents the Communion of the Apostles (Pl. XXXII). The faithful receives communion standing before or below this icon and contemplating it, he is led to see the royal table of God in heaven. Taken in its entirety the iconostasis shows the history of salvation. On the royal doors, the Four Evangelists remind the believer of the message of the Gospels; the Annunciation brings the divine in contact with the human; it means also the entry into Paradise, symbolized by the sanctuary to which these doors lead. Presupposition of this entry, however, is the faithful's participation in the Sacrament, indicated in the icon of the Communion of the Apostles, the understanding and acceptance of the mystery of the Incarnation and the results of it, revealed on the feast icons and those above them.

The meaning of the iconostasis is, therefore, not only didactic and symbolic, but it parallels the interpretation of the liturgy. The believer participates in a very tangible way in the communion of saints and the glory of the kingdom, when he kisses and venerates the icons of the lower row. Even the metal covers placed on many of these icons, the *oklad*, stress the transcendental character of the represented figure and remove the holy from everyday reality. In the last analysis the iconostasis is not a "symbol" or an "object of devotion"; it is the gate through which this world is bound to the other. The people, through these icons, participate in it and are transferred into the divine world.[20]

The liturgy comprises other elements which have left their impact on the iconography of the icons, while hymns and psalms chanted in the liturgy have increased the repertory of icon painting. They have contributed to the creation of some symbolic, didactic themes like the "Let every living creature...", or even to the repertory of Mariolatry, to mention two important categories of subjects derived from worship (Pls. XLV-XLVIII).

ICONS AND THE SACRAMENTS

The icon plays a role in sacraments and *sacramentals*, that is, actions in the church which possess a sacramental character, although the use of the icon for the performance of any of them is not prescribed. For example, Confession is often heard in front of an icon or the faithful would pray in front of an icon of the Mother of God before he begins his confession. If the penitent does not face the iconostasis, he faces a desk on which are placed the cross or an icon of the Saviour or the Gospels. The words of the priest stress the presence

---

[18] Migne, *PG*, 155, 345.
[19] Bulgakov, S., *L'Orthodoxie*, Paris 1932, translates the word "sobornost" as "ecumenical".
[20] Leeuw van der, G., *Liturgik?*, Nijkerk 1946; Id., *Sacred and Profane Beauty*, London 1963, pp. 173, 174.

of Christ through the icon: "Christ stands here invisibly and receives your confession...
see, his holy icon is before us..." [21] An icon, in Athens, illustrates the sacrament of Confession, its effects on the penitent. Healed from the poisons of his sins represented as snakes, freed from the tortures of hell depicted below, he is reconciled with the Church, which brings great joy to the Heavens (Pl. XXXVII).

Although the use of icons is not prescribed in the Euchologion, their presence in the performance of sacraments is to be understood, for in some old manuscripts relevant rubrics have survived. For instance, in the service performed for the Engagement in the church, one reads that a small table has been arranged on which an icon has been placed with tapers on either side. The priest censes the holy icon "and the newly engaged and all those present." [22] And again at the ceremony of blessing a woman forty days after the birth of her child, "the priest takes oil from the lamp burning before the icon of Mary and makes the sign of the cross on the child's face." If the child is a girl the ceremony is performed in front of the iconostasis while for the boy it takes place around the altar.[23] In the Baptism the priest censes cross-wise the water in the baptismal font and the holy icons and the entire church and those present. The last contact a man makes with an icon is at his funeral. Notice the icon of Christ resting on the body of St. Ephraim the Syrian (Pl. XXXb).

Icons have also other functions in the church. Miraculous icons and events associated with them have their own feast days in the Church calendar. On such days the icon is carried in procession through the city or from one church to the next. There exist special *processional*, bilateral icons for this purpose (Pl. VIc). Processions of icons also take place in cases of *litanies*, prayers of an entire community. The icon is carried through the city or in the battle field to prevent, protect or deliver the city from natural or human catastrophes (Pl. XLIa). Legends about such icons continue to this day throughout the Eastern Church and often have political implications which belong to a vast topic that cannot be discussed in this book.

ICONOGRAPHY

Themes in General

In attempting to understand the themes of icons, their specific content and meaning, that is, their iconography, we must consider the themes themselves in general and the way they are represented in particular. Their treatment reveals changes which in their turn embody theological ideas. There are icons depicting scenes—histories—taken from the Old and New Testaments, the Apocrypha, the heroic deeds of the martyrs, or deriving from mystical writings, liturgical interpretations and church hymns. Other icons contain holy portraits only. In other words, the themes of the icons are the great themes of Christianity, that is the Incarnation of God and its meaning for man.

Man, son of God by adoption, made in the image and likeness of God, born in immortality, fell from it willingly into the darkness of non-being and death. Man had to be revived and by right of his birth, become participant in the glory of God, that is, to attain his deification. This was achieved by the divine descent—the Incarnation—and the human ascent. The Incarnation is shown in representations of Christ and his Mother and its mysteries are

[21] Ware, T., *The Orthodox Church*, Penquin Books 1963, p. 296.
[22] Trempelas, P. N., *Mikron Euchologion*, i, Athens 1950, p. 29.
[23] *Ibid.*, pp. 330, 347, 348.

manifested in the twelve Great Feasts of the Church (Pls XI-XX). Themes from the Old Testament, seen as prefigurations of the New, are also common. The Hospitality of Abraham for example, becomes a symbol of the Holy Trinity (Pl. IVa). The prophet Elijah is associated with Christ's Transfiguration for his prayer to see the face of God was fulfilled on Mount Thabor, where he saw the uncreated light of God (Pl. X).

The possibility of deliverance from corruption was not confined to those who witnessed the Incarnation or received its message through the Gospels. Christ descended into Hell and brought deliverance to all. The richness of thought manifested in the theme of the Anastasis, the Descent into Hell, can be understood by comparing Eastern icons with Western representations of the Resurrection, portraying Christ simply rising from the grave. In the Anastasis, Christ, the new Adam, lifts Adam and Eve whose deliverance was foretold by the prophet kings and preached to the dead by John the Baptist (Pl. XVIII).

Man has fallen into sin and deliverance is necessary. Here Eastern Christianity has an important idea to present. It emphasizes the freedom of human will which is beautifully illustrated on icons related to the Lives of the Saints. Ascetics, founders of monasteries or hermits in the desert left all they had, and seeking God put themselves to all kinds of tests and hardships. Their struggles are triumphs of human will. Their images on icons are symbols of their consuming desire for the consumation of their love for Christ (Pls. XXVIII-XXXI). Their struggles revealed to man the meaning of the good fight for Christ (Pl. XXXa); they led him to accept suffering in life and the mystery of death which is suggested on icons mainly by a sense of peace permeating Dormition scenes, such as the Falling Asleep of St. Ephraim the Syrian, a popular subject during the last period of Byzantine art (Pl. XXXb).

Even on the Day of Judgement, when man would appear before the throne of the Lord to be judged, he would find intercessors: the Mother of God, St. John the Baptist. The river of fire, and the torments of the sinners are opposed by the bliss of Paradise. The Mother of God would plead to her Son for "his sons." [24] It is out of this need that so many variants of the Mother of God as intercessor have appeared on icons (Pl. VIIa). But, after all, the entire Church intercedes for humanity and the doctrine of the Intercession of the Saints is pictorialized in icons of the Deesis (Pls. XI, XXXIIIa).

Incarnation, sin and repentance, life of good fight are stations on the great journey leading to man's union with God and his entry into the glory of light, a possibility stressed by the Greek, Syrian and Russian fathers. Union with Christ is achieved by every member of the Church which is the body of Christ. The believer is united with Christ through the sacraments. The icons of the Communion of the Apostles, already discussed, indicate this union and emphasize the Sacrament. So does another icon portraying Mary of Egypt receiving her last communion from Father Zosimas (Pl. XXXVc).

The ascent, however, leading to a union with God has obstacles. It is a struggle pictorialized in the theme of the *Heavenly Ladder*, illustrating the treatise of John Climacus, which icon painters borrowed from illustrated manuscripts. Devils push the monks down the ladder, the rungs of which are the virtues securing the ascent, but on top of the ladder is Christ to receive and to crown those who persist (Pl. XXXa).

---

[24] Galavaris, G., "Mary's Descent into Hell," *Byzantine Studies/Etudes byzantines*, 4 (1977), 189-194.

When man becomes one with the divinity—Eastern mystics describe the states of ascent in detail—he is illuminated by the uncreated light revealed in Christ's Transfiguration (Pls. XI, XXXI), and assumes the likeness of the transfigured body of Christ. The divine penetrates the human and man achieves knowledge of God. By knowing God man acquires a knowledge of the creation because all that exists, exists in Him. Isaac of Nineveh (sixth century) describes this knowledge as a "cosmic sight" that is man sees everything as spirit and embraces all with his love.[25] On icons there are specific subjects representing the harmony of the universe around the Lord which derive from liturgical texts such as the "Let every living creature praise the Lord..." or from the Lives of the Saints. Notice, for example, St. Gerasimus who journeys to the funeral of St. Ephraim riding a lion (Pl. XXXb); in other instances he converses with it.[26] Above all, it is through the transformed landscape and the aesthetic language of the icon that one sees the world revealed in its future state. In representations of the Nativity, for example, one witnesses the spiritual triumph of the creation (Pls. XI, XIV).

The Iconography of the Themes

The themes have taken fixed forms and are recognized everywhere. However, one can observe changes, more so in the rendering of the "histories" and less in the holy portraits which best present the likeness of the prototype and render as far as this is possible the features and character of the saints as described in the Lives of the Saints and in the manuals which came to codify the oral tradition. The general principle determining the representations of holy portraits is frontality and in general a hieratic quality. The "histories", whether related to Christ or to the saints, are represented in their essentials so as to make their message clear. In this way icons parallel the Gospel and the liturgical texts. Events and portraits are depicted as ever present just as they are made ever present in the liturgy. Nevertheless, there are icons telling a story in a narrative way, that is, more than one episode is contained in a panel, presented in consecutive phases. We can see, for example, the icon of the Sacrifice of Abraham, in Athens, showing the departure of Isaac from his home (lower right part of the picture), the sacrifice in all details on the upper part, and finally the return home in the central part, (Pl. VIII) On other icons the episodes are grouped according to liturgical and dogmatic principles, as in the case of the Twelve Great Feasts. These principles remained basically unaltered throughout the centuries although the iconography itself was enriched with details that made the represented episodes more life-like. This is true of the Palaeologan period, the last phase of the Byzantine Empire (13th-15th centuries) and for the Post-Byzantine icon-painting in the Greek world particularly in Crete whose painters introduced new types such as the Holy Trinity in which all three Persons are represented (Pl. IVc), or at times compositions borrowed from Italian engravings (Pl. XVIc). In the Slavic world the iconography is enriched by the introduction of local saints such as St. Nicholas of Mozahjsk (Pl. XXVIIc), Basil the Fool (Pl. XXIXc), by themes related to local wonder icons and legends and by subjects of a didactic, mystic nature, like the Glorification of the Pure Soul (Pl. XXXVIIIa).

---

[25] Wensinck, A. J., Trans., *Mystic Treatises by Isaac of Nineveh Translated from Bedjan's Syrian Text* (Verhandelingen der Koninklijke Akademie van Wetenschappen, Afdeeling Letterkunde n.s. XXIII), Amsterdam 1923, p. 341.
[26] See, for example, a 16th century Russian Icon in Onasch, K., *Ikonen*, Gütersloh 1961, pl. 120.

Icons of Christ and the Trinity

Christ's icon depicts Him as the God-Man, according to the doctrine of Chalcedon. It represents the Person of the Son of God who became man, consubstantial with the Father by His divine nature, and consubstantial to man by His human nature.

The types of Christ on icons are not numerous. The most common and earliest type is that of Christ Pantocrator, the Almighty or He who holds everything in His hand; at the same time the Saviour, the Lover of Man, the Merciful—these epithets often appear on icons. He is frontally represented with long hair and beard in bust form or seated on a throne holding a gospel in one hand and blessing with the other. Often the expression of the face, through the hands of great artists, like the one who created the encaustic icon in Sinai, can convey the attributes of Christ (Pl. Ia). In this icon Christ is the Lover of Man and the Merciful. The faithful can promise to this Christ that "we shall walk forever in the light of the glory of thy face." [27] Other types which appear, except for the young, beardless, Christ-Emmanuel, can be considered in fact variants of the Pantocrator type. Their origins should be sought mainly in the liturgy, such as "He who sitteth on the Cherubim," the enthroned Pantocrator whose throne is carried by the symbols of the Evangelists and is surrounded by the Seraphim and the Cherubim, a type that has appeared in the pre-iconoclastic period [28] (Pl. II). Here Christ is the "Creator of every creature visible and invisible whom the heavens and the heavens of heavens praise ...," [29] the immutable one for whom "a thousand years are but as yesterday when it is past," (Ps. 88[89]: 4).

Likewise the type of Christ as the High Priest, most popular in post-byzantine icons, has liturgical origins, as we have already pointed out. Its liturgical character is stressed even more in Deesis' compositions as we see, for example, in the Greek triptych now in Madison, Wisconsin (Pl. XI).

Although actual models for some of these types should be sought in Hellenistic portrayals of divinities, such as Zeus or Asclepius, tradition has it that the features of Christ on these icons go back to miraculously formed images such as the cloth of Kamuliana in Cappadocia, rescued from a water-basin in the garden of a pagan woman about 540, and the Syrian Mandylion, acquired by the King Abgarus of Edessa, and transferred to Constantinople in 944 to be lost later. The Mandylion was distinguished by the expression of Christ which could be meek and austere at the same time. It was copied on icons and became popular in the seventeenth and eighteenth centuries. In one of the icons chosen here the Mandylion is shown as the *acheiropoietos* portrait, *vera icon*, and in another bilateral icon it is related to the Adoration of the Cross depicted on the reverse side; but in an icon in Sinai the Edessa legend is depicted in a narrative way. The Apostle Taddaeus delivers the wonder image to King Abgarus who was healed by it. This iconography of the Mandylion developed in Constantinople, disseminated in other parts of the Empire and reached Russia [30] (Pl. III).

Man represents on icons that which is revealed to him; Jesus, the Holy Ghost in the

---

[27] *Triodion*, p. 77.

[28] Galavaris, G., *The Illustrations of the Prefaces in Byzantine Gospels* (Bizantina Vindobonensia, XI), Vienna 1979, pp. 73[ff].

[29] From the Liturgy of the Syrian Jacobites, Brightman, F. E., *Liturgies Eastern and Western*, 1, Oxford 1896, repr. 1965, p. 85.

[30] Velthuis, B., *De Zoon, Christus op Ikonen*, Echteld 1980, pp. 50[ff].

form of a dove, or the tongues of fire in Pentecost. The three Persons of the Trinity are
first shown symbolically through Old Testament episodes. According to liturgical texts,
the Three Hebrews in the Fire prefigured the Trinity and the Incarnation of Christ (Pl.
IX).[31] But a more common symbolic representation of the Holy Trinity is the Hospitality
of Abraham, never forgotten on Greek and Russian icons (Pl. IVa). Nevertheless, artists
found ways of representing all three Persons of the Holy Trinity. First in the so-called
Synthronoi and *Paternitas* type, a theme not known on icons earlier than the fourteenth
century, and the so-called "Western" Trinity first found in Cretan icons of the sixteenth
century (Pl. IV).

The Mother of God

The Saviour of the world was born of a Virgin. Her image holding the infant child became the most common subject on icons. Mary's iconographic types depending on wonder-
icons and on legends have multiplied so much that we cannot even list the types here
although many of them are variants of certain basic types derived from famous icons.[32]
Certainly one of the most celebrated icons is the *Hodegetria* (Pointing the Way) portraying
the Virgin holding the infant Christ on her right or left arm. According to tradition it was
painted by St. Luke and became the palladium of Constantinople (Pl. V).

Other icons emphasize more directly the reality of the Incarnation. The *Galactotrophousa*
is the mother who feeds her child, a type popular among Italo-Byzantine masters. It
declares that now "He who showered down upon the desert manna for the people/With
milk from a woman's breast is fed." [33] This image is also found in some beuatiful pieces of
apocryphal literature, like the Syriac, *The Vision of Theophilus* describing the sojourn
of the holy family in Egypt: "... and I (Mary) was left under the tree feeding from my
breasts my Son on whom was a garment of the colour of a grape ... and the colour of the
sandals of my son resembled the colour of golden silver on his feet ..." [34] The *Blachernitissa*, the Mother of God praying and with the child Christ in a medallion on her breast,
known also with other epithets and variants, based on a famous marble icon in the Blachernae Church in Constantinople, is the *par excellence* Incarnation icon. Its meaning is made
clear in the twelfth/thirteenth century Russian icon known as the *"Ustuig"* Annunciation (Pl. XIIb). The Greek icon became the model for an icon in Novgorod which saved
the city from the attack of Suzdalians. Several other copies were made and the type became known as Znamenje, the Virgin of the Sign (Pl. VIc).

In other icons it is the suffering awaiting the Mother of God that is stressed. While
she holds the Child against her breast, Archangels are flying down, carrying the symbols
of the Passion. Known as the Virgin "The Symbols of the Passion" the type relates to
church-hymns, although the nucleus of the concept comes from Luke 2:35. The theme,
not known, fully developed at least, on icons of the Byzantine period, was favoured by the

---

[31] See *sticheron* of Sunday before Christmas, *To Hagion Dodekaemeron*, 1, Athens 1978 (Apostolike
Diakonia), pp. 10, 11.

[32] Velthuis, B., et al., *Ikon-Maria*, Echteld 1979 (very usufel for the various legends related to icons
and the "types" they represent).

[33] Sophronios of Jerusalem (d. 638), Migne, *PG*, 87, III, 4008.

[34] Mingana, A., Trans., *The Vision of Theophilus* (Woodbrooke Studies, III), Cambridge 1931,
pp. 19-21.

Creto-Venetian painters from the fifteenth to the seventeenth century (Pl. VIa).[35]

Through her role in the Incarnation, Mary can intercede to her Son for humanity. Romanos the Melodist (sixth century) in his canticle on the Nativity, I, presents the Mother of God saying, "... I am not feeding you the Giver of milk with milk of sheer fortuity ... I beseech you for all mankind ... for through me who has given birth ... (men) will return and feel again the beauty of paradise," [36] There are icons depicting her as "orans" known by various epithets. The thirteenth century Freising icon, chosen here, although it belongs to this group, has a liturgical foundation as the accompanying inscription makes clear. She is "the hope of the despaired ones," an appelation found often in liturgical texts. According to legend this icon is a copy of one painted by Luke. It reached Milan as a present of the Emperor John Palaeologuss (1341-1391) and finally it was sent to Freising on September 23rd 1440. Liturgical is also the sixth-seventh century tapestry-icon in Cleveland (Pl. VII). Mary, like an empress, flanked by her bodyguards, the angels, displays the infant Christ to the onlooker. She is surrounded by the Apostles who brought the message of the Word to the world. Above her is a representation of Christ in the form of a liturgical *Majestas*. The Incarnation is stressed once more but in a fuller theological way taking the form of an Epiphany.

It was from the dogma, the liturgy, exegeses and the piety of people, that a pictorial cycle was developed which was very popular on icons, and was related to the cult and glorification of Mary (Pls. XLV-XLVIII). Legends of miraculous icons, parallelisms to Christ, themes borrowed from His iconography, are part of this cycle which ends with Mary's Coronation. In the Orthodox tradition, however, Mary never sits on the same throne with her Son, as she does in Western art, which nevertheless penetrated Eastern piety. At least one example, an icon from the Crusaders' period, found in the monastery of Mount Sinai, shows this (Pl. XLVIIb).

The Great Feasts

In order to stress the dogma and the liturgy, Byzantine theologians chose twelve events from the life of Christ—this number is not always followed—associated with the great Church Festivals which had become part of a programme of church decoration that was crystallized after the triumph of the icons. The compositions of these twelve feasts the *dodekaortion*- took their standard form probably in the tenth century resulting from scenes selected from the narrative Gospels and following an arrangement which reflects liturgical practices. Icons with these feasts were placed on the upper part of the iconostasis, as we have already pointed out, although their use as devotional icons is also known. Because of their liturgical and dogmatic character, iconographic changes of the Great Feasts are limited, although questions of expression, that is style, always follow different paths depending on the locality, the date, and of course, the artist. On the whole the iconography of these feasts is similar to that found in works of monumental art and book illumination.

The Annunciation Feast is exemplified in a number of icons which can demonstrate

---

[35] Cf. Sotiriou, Maria, "Panagia tou Pathous. Vizantine eikona tes Mones Sina," *Panegyrikos 1400 amphieteridi tes Hieras Mones Sina*, Athens 1969, pp. 29-42.

[36] Maas, P., and Trypanis, A., Eds., *Romanos, Cantica genuina*, Oxford 1963, pp. 8. 9.

iconographic changes and their meaning.[37] The icon in Sinai comes closer to the Luke account (1:28) which indicates a salutation and Annunciation in a dwelling, while the spinning may come from one of the two apocryphal texts from the Proto-Evangelium of James. The Holy Ghost descending from heaven in the form of a dove is a symbol of divine visitation. The message of the Incarnation is destined for all mankind, it radiates beyond the personages represented on the icon. For "today is the beginning of our salvation and the revelation of the Mystery which is for eternity," the *troparion* of the festival proclaims.[38] It is not without significance that plants, birds and a river have been represented in the foreground for the creatures are subjected to this message also. The entire meaning of the Incarnation is stressed more in the Tretyakov Gallery-icon, already referred to, which contains only the essentials. The Virgin appears as if displaying the infant Child "conceived by the Holy Ghost." The dogmatic meaning is further stressed by the representation of Christ seated on the Cherubim, above. But, in the seventeenth century Annunciation, the icon from Yaroslav, the composition is richer in narrative details (Pl. XIII).

The Annunciation meant the revelation of the Mystery, the actual birth meant the "revelation of knowledge." In Nativity icons the main theme is the birth of the God-Man placed in the center of the composition.[39] Here "in a crib reclines God, he who made real the firmament from the beginning." [40] Supplementary episodes deriving from the Gospel of Luke, 2:4-20, and the Apocryphal Evangelium of James (third-fourth century, 17:17[ff]), are grouped around it: the Bathing of the Child, the Journey and/or the Adoration of the Magi which have been included in some compositions because the Adoration is celebrated by the Church on Christmas day. In the twelfth-century Sinai icon although the emphasis is on the Nativity, a fact revealing the liturgical character of the icon, the liturgical element is stressed further by the depiction of the angelic choirs. The icon has retained earlier narrative elements from the Apocrypha of James and Pseudo-Matthew, depicting episodes following the divine birth: the Dream of Joseph, the Flight into and Arrival in Egypt, the Escape of Elizabeth with the infant John, the Massacre of the Innocents.[41] That is, we see here episodes from the infancy of Christ commemorated by the Church on December 25 and 29 (Pl. XIV). Other icons represent a more standarized type: the thoughtful Joseph tempted by the old shepherd, who came to be the Devil transformed into a shepherd, becomes a typical element of Eastern iconography (Pl. XI).

Icons with the Baptism demonstrate the two natures of Christ as formulated in Chalcedon in 451. The descending dove emphasizes the divine nature of Christ, but the angels holding robes to cover Christ refer to His human nature. In a fourteenth-century rendering of this scene there is a grouping and inflation of episodes deriving from the Gospels around the principal baptism scene: John baptizing the Jews (Mk 1:4, 5)—the groups standing on either side of the river's shores, those swimming in the streams of the Jordan, personified by an ancient personification, and the meeting of John with Christ (Mt 3:13-15). The grouping of these episodes has a purely liturgical character; it is based on readings

---

[37] Schiller, G., *Ikonographie der christlichen Kunst*, 1, Gütersloh 1966, pp. 44[ff].
[38] Dennis, C. P. L., Trans., *A Manual of Eastern Orthodox Prayers*, London 1945, p. 139.
[39] Schiller, *op. cit.* pp. 76-77.
[40] Sophronios of Jerusalem, Migne, *PG*, 87, III, 4008
[41] Schiller, *op. cit.*, pp. 127[ff].

used on the eve and on the festival day and it reflects lectionary illustrations.[42] But the opening of the heavens above by the angels refers to hymns chanted on the occasion such as, to mention only one example, the *troparion* by Cosmas Maiuma (eighth century) for the Eve of the Epiphany; "the universe rejoices, the heavens too, the angels sing melodious hymns ... Christ is coming to save all that exists in the streams of the Jordan" [43] (Pl. XV).

In other festival icons, iconographic changes tend to make the event more vivid and add a tone of drama as we see, for example, in the Faising of Lazarus. Martha and Mary may beseech Christ on their knees or they may stand, covering their noses (Pl. XV); or the landscape can play an important part as it does in the depiction of the Transfiguration.[44] Its typical rendering includes only the main personages, but at times it can be expanded with narrative episodes depicting the ascent and descent of the group to and from Mount Thabor (Pl. XXXI). The "light" of the transfigured Lord acquired a special meaning through the theology of the *Hesychasts* in the fourteenth century. Their leader, Gregory Palamas, proclaimed that the "uncreated light" could be perceived through contemplation. This doctrine brought about iconographic changes especially in the rendering of the Glory of Christ and gave a special place to the icon of the Transfiguration in the Orthodox world.

The iconography of the Crucifixion adheres either to a strict dogmatic rendering of the scene comprising the protagonists—Mary and the beloved disciple, or to a narrative, crowded composition expressing a desire for the Christian's participation in the drama. In these renderings a spirit of majesty alternates with dramatic outcries of pain and suffering of all participants. In essence these images reflect the liturgy of the Passion week: "in vain winged servants, full of tears, turn around him. They cannot help his suffering ... He who is more beautiful than mortal men is seen now dead ... 'Who will give me water and open fountains of tears— thus the Virgin wept, the Bride of God—so that I may shed tears for my sweet Jesus?'" Some of the most beautiful liturgical poetry that Eastern man has produced is chanted in front of such icons on Good Friday (Pl. XVI).

The sufferings of the cross are unthinkable without the light of the Resurrection, the Anastasis. In early Christian art the Resurrection of Christ was represented by the visit of the three Marys to the Tomb (Mt 28:1[f]; Mk 16:1-8; Lk 24:1-10). On the earliest icons, we have the appearance of Christ to the two Marys known as the Chairete which follows the narrative of the Gospels except that the Mother of God, not mentioned in the Gospels, takes the place of the mother of James. The Chairete has survived on icons of all periods with variations (Pl. XVII).[45] The Hann Collection icon, for example, shows a conflation of the visit to the Tomb and the Appearance of Christ to the Marys. The soldiers are multiplied and are dressed in costumes recalling Medieval representations of battle scenes (Pl. XVIIa).

---

[42] Galavaris, G., *The Illustrations of the Liturgical Homilies of Gregory Nazianzenus*, Princeton, N.J., 1969, pp. 87[ff].

[43] Pitra, J. B., Ed., *Analecta sacra, Spicilegio solesmensi parata*, 1, Paris 1876, pp. 418[ff].

[44] Schiller, *op. cit.*, pp. 155[ff].

[45] Weitzmann, K., "Eine vorikonoklastische Ikone des Sinai mit der Darstellung des Chairete," *Tortulae, Römische Quartalschrift für christliche Altertumskunde und Kirchegeschichte*, 30, Supplementheft, pp. 317-327.

But the principal feast picture of the Resurrection on Greek and Russian icons is the Anastasis, the Descent into Hell, a scene based on the apocryphal gospel of Nicodemus. It is one of the most important Christological scenes, for it portrays the exact moment of redemption: "He lifts up mortals from their graves and the depths of their sins," and so is "Adam healed." The victory over death, the trampling down of death, is always portrayed in the centre foreground. Hades could not endure Christ's presence, "he was blinded by the glory of His light" and is now chained, while the chains of those who were Hade's prisoners are broken so that they can hasten to life. Different iconographic renderings, depending on the action of Christ occur in icons as they do in book illumination and monumental art and express dogmatic nuances. Since the fourteenth century the relation of the Resurrection to the Passion has generally been shown through the introduction of angels carrying the Passion Symbols in the scene (Pl. XVIII). The persons were also multiplied and other episodes expanding the dogmatic meaning of the great event were introduced.[46] This is often the case in Russian Easter icons from the seventeenth century on, exemplified by an icon in West Berlin (Pl. XIXa). On the lower half of the icon one sees the Descent into Hell and several persons proceeding upwards to Paradise; Peter diving into the sea to reach the resurrected Christ is shown on the lower right (Jn 21:7-8); at the door of heavens above right, stands the good thief carrying his cross, shown once more within the City of God where he is welcomed by Elijah and Elisha; in the upper centre, the risen Christ points to the archangel who chains Hades and whose pride "is abolished by the mighty one." Peter overlooks from the roof of a building above. The entire composition is crowned by a representation of the Holy Trinity. The dogmatic implications and the relations of these supplementary episodes to the Easter liturgy are well known.

The dogma has also contributed to the iconography of the Ascension (Mk 16:19; Lk 24:50-53; Ac. 1:9-12), one of the oldest dogmatic compositions which may have its model in a monumental representation in Palestine. Neither Mary nor Paul is mentioned in the written account. Mary's presence emphasized the two natures of Christ who carries His humanity to heaven, while Paul stands as a representative of the Church born of the gentiles. On icons, this composition remains fundamentally unaltered (Pl. XIXb). This is also true for the Pentecost scene although changes are sometimes found as the icon in Athos shows (Pl. XIXc). Here the space left empty for the invisible presence of the Word of God, between the two groups of Apostles, is now occupied by Mary. This is an important iconography in the context of Mariology. A similar question is raised by the Dormition of the Virgin or *Koimesis* which often closes the cycle of the twelve feasts. Based on the apocrypha of the Assumption of the Virgin, it reflects a monumental standarized composition. The earliest extant example on icons is an eleventh-century icon in Sinai depicting the theme in its basic elements, in a composition that is repeated in later Greek and Russian icons (Pl. XX): the Apostles, except Thomas, are gathered around the bier of Mary, while Christ appeared amidst them to take Mary's soul to heaven. Later, an iconography is developed which includes other episodes, taken from the apocrypha such as the story of the defiant Jew, Jephonias, more descriptive details and a complex architecture (Pl.XXb).

---

[46] Lange, R., *Die Auferstehung*, Recklinghausen 1966.

The receiving of the soul means the return of Mary to her original condition, her entrance to Paradise spiritually. Therefore this is one of the most important representations in the Mariology cycle.

Angels and Saints

Among the Church feasts a special place is given to the Feast of the *Synaxis* of the Archangels and of all the heavenly powers, celebrated on November 8. This is the feast dedicated to the spirits sent to serve "those who shall inherit salvation" (Heb. 1:14). The choir of angels are constantly participating in the heavenly liturgy, surrounding God's altar and throne. They are at His service, a role manifested on icons in various ways. Angels bear testimony of Christ's Incarnation, in the Baptism scene; or they participate in the lament of the universe at the hour of the cross; they are the guardians of the Christians who ask God in their prayers "fence us around with thy holy angels." The Church, however, places particular emphasis on Gabriel and Michael, "the captains and leaders of the armies of heaven." Gabriel, meaning "Power of God" is the special messanger of God's will. On a Russian icon standing before the throne of God, Gabriel receives the message, then leaving the celestial realm, arrives on earth and delivers the message to Mary (Pl. XIIIb). But it is Michael "who is like God," the exalted warrior and glorious victor who turns aside the evil.

In an icon chosen here, Michael is shown in a celebrated miracle performed at Chonai in Phrygia, commemorated by the Church on September 6. Michael with his javelin arrested the river flood, caused by pagans and saved his hermitage and the monk Archippos who served there. The archangel guided the water to an underground channel into which "the river still flows and vanishes to this day," (Pl. XXIc). It is also Michael who protects the faithful, the Church from "all the snares and wiles of the Devil... from the darts and the destructive rage of the demons." As the horseman of the celestial army carrying a spear or a sword, Michael, the Herald of the Apocalypse, defends the Church crushing the Antichrist, the Devil and his kingdom, in the name of the Incarnate Christ represented in the upper right hand corner of the icon. The bust of Christ, the altar with the Gospels and the Eucharistic chalice on it show once more the impact of the liturgy (Pl. XXId). This theme had a wide dissemination on Russian icons.

The Church comprises that which is visible and invisible, the living and the dead. Her saints form an unbroken chain. Saint Symeon, the New Theologian, says that the saints "become a golden chain in which each saint is a separate link united to the next by faith, works and love" (Centuries, III, 2-4). The Eastern Christian prays to the saints who therefore have a place on icons. It may be a holy portrait or an episode from their lives or both. A subject which recurrs on icons since the fifteenth century is the Ecstatic Meeting of Peter and Paul, known in other media since earlier centuries, or Peter and Paul holding a model of the Church, known on icons not before the sixteenth century, both expressing the belief in and the desire for the unity of the Church (Pls. XXII, XXIIIab). The concept of the apostolic succession and continuity of tradition is manifested in themes like St. John Chrysostom, the Fountain of Wisdom (Pl. XXIV). Source of his wisdom is Paul and recipients of its streams are John's followers. The saints' martyrdom is found often on calendar icons, illustrated menologia, comprising the lives of the saints for each month (Pl. XXVI). Some saints enjoy greater popularity than others, the result of special popular piety, such as St. Demetrius and above all St. George, bearer of light, patron of farmers and herdsmen. This is how the Russian people invoked him in one of their songs: "We have gone around the field/We have called Yegory/'Oh thou, our brave Yegory/ Save our cattle,/In the field and beyond the field." [47] For the Christian iconographer he remains the dragon-slayer (Pl. XXV). And yet neither he nor St. Demetrius were always represented on horses slaying the dragon or the enemy. Their earliest representations on icons show them standing frontally.

Other saints appear on icons of distinct popular character. One of them is St. Christopher the Dog-Headed (Cynocephalos) whose icons, known since the fifteenth century, remind us of the Christianization of the Egyptian god Anubis, or the exorcism of evil through magic and the use of animal masks (Pl. XXVIIa).[48]

There are also holy portraits of ascetics—and these are the ones which remain faithful to the tradition—, stylites and founders of monastic communities: St. Onuphrius the Anchorite, who was discovered by Apa Papnout in the desert (fourth century) "naked, his hair covered him and served as clothing for him." [49] But the Greek writers of his Life preferred to see him covered also with green leaves, and so he appears on icons; St. Simeon the Stylite the Elder (d. 459), the most famous of pillar saints, the counsellor of countless pilgrims, the "peace-maker of the desert;" St. Euthymius the Great, one of the most venerated monks in fifth century Palestine and his pupil the Abbot Sabas, the founder of the famous Lavra in a wild gorge between Jerusalem and the Dead Sea, one who had an important influence on the development of Easter monasticism; the bishop Sava (d. 1235), the parton saint of the Serbian people, founder of the Khilandari monastery on Mount Athos. These holy portraits on icons remain unaltered as symbols of the ideals of monasticism, especially as exemplified by the Hesychasts, and bear a perpetual testimony to the fire set in one's heart by the love of God (Pls. XXVIII, XXIX).

The iconography of the themes as we have attempted to suggest, owes a great deal to the liturgy whose impact is further shown in a group of didactic, mystical icons. Their iconographic foundations are manifold. It can be a prayer recited in the liturgy such as the "Our Father" or "In the Name of the Father and the Son." It can be a Gospel verse of an allegorical character, taken over by liturgical poetry and amplified by a series of mystical images in theological writings. For example, this is the case of the theme Christ the Vine. In Greek icons it forms a literal representation of the verse "I am the vine tree and you are the branches" (Jn 15:5) with a direct reference to the Church as stated in liturgical prayers. In the Rumanian glass icon it becomes a pure symbol of the Eucharistic sacrifice, "the cup of the fruit of the vine" (Liturgy of St. Basil) (Pl. XXXIVc).

Liturgical poetry as another source of iconography, can be mentioned here. The hymns, for instance, of the third Sunday of Lent (Feast of the Adoration of the Cross), of Good Friday and of the Feast of the Exaltation of the Cross (September 14) provided the textual basis for the theme of the "Glorification" of the Cross (Pl. XXXIIIc). Poetry related to the Passion cycle can also be singled out as another example. To this belong the type of Christ "The Image of Pity" (Pl. XXXVa), representing Christ naked, half-figure, in the grave with a cross behind it, and its Russian relative "Mother weep not for me" in which

[47] Ralston, W. S. R., *The Songs of the Russian People*, London 1872, p. 230.
[48] *Kunst der Ostkirche*, Stift Herzogenburg, Exhibition Catalogue, Vienna 1977, pp. 324-325.
[49] Wallis Budge, E., Trans., *Egyptian Tales and Romances*, London 1931, p. 264.

the half-buried Christ gives the promise of the Resurrection to His Mother, a theme popular in late Russian icons. Through icons the theme has left its impact on literature. Anna Akhmatova's moving "Crucifixion" in her *Requiem*, is based on such an icon.[50] To the same cycle belongs the beautiful icon in Patmos portraying the Lamentation (Pl. XXXIVa). It represents an iconography crystallized in the fourteenth century under strong liturgical impact and influences of representations of the same theme in textiles.

Still the iconography of a theme can be given a different meaning through variations in its rendering. The theme of Christ "Image of Pity," for example, can attain a direct eucharistic significance under the impact of the liturgy. An eucharistic chalice takes the place of the grave. This means that Christ is not only the "Image of Pity", the King of Glory, but above all the Bread of Life. Icons following this rendering declare that "this bread (is) indeed the precious body of our Lord..." and "in this cup (is) the precious blood of Christ" (Liturgy of St. Basil, Anaphora) (Pl. XXXVb).

In other instances, a text of a mystic nature can be so elaborate that its pictorial rendering cannot be understood unless the text is cited on the panel as it is on the icon of the Glorification of the Pure Soul, now in Vienna (Pl. XXXVIIIa). In fact the composition is an illustration of the text inscribed on it, whose translation is: "the pure Soul as Virgin adorned with every flower stands before the sun; the moon lies under her feet, a prayer comes out of her mouth like a flame and reaches the heavens and over the heavens beyond. With her tears she wipes out the sins of the world, tames the lions, calms down the dragons with her goodness. The Devil submits himself to her and no longer can endure the human and divine goodness." Since the middle of the sixteenth century these text-illustrations on icons have become popular in Russia, especially in Moscow.

Icons and Popular Piety

Worship influences the personal lives of the worshippers who may not always understand the theological nuances of the doctrine. And this is true for the icon whose theology and the Platonic ideas which shaped it have little effect on the people who continue to see it not as a reflection of the divine but as a holy object to be prayed and spoken to and to be worshiped like relics of saints. The personal encounter with the icon has contributed much to its dissemination. Icons are found in houses, private chapels, at the crossroads, they are carried by believers around their necks or in their travels. At baptism an Orthodox is given the name of a saint "as a symbol of his entry into the unity of the Church," retains a special devotion to the saint whose name he bears and has an icon with him for his private devotions. A large number of icons with holy portraits are *votive* icons of this type. They represent patron saints or miracles which have a special meaning for the individual. A case in point is the Russian icon in the National Gallery of Canada (Pl. XXVIIb).

This human element has contributed to the iconography. If one were to discuss the various iconographic types of the Mother of God from this point of view, their humanity, no matter how closely interwoven with the doctrine of the Incarnation, one would confront all gamuts of human feelings: calm grandeur; melancholic serenity; tenderness; suffering and compassion. A study also of the epithets found on Mary's icons would contribute much to understanding feelings of piety. In what terms, for example, would

---

[50] For an English translation see McKane, R., *Anna Akhmatova, Selected Poems*, Penguin Books 1969, p. 102.

one interpret the epithet *heliocalos*, "beautiful like the son," given to Mary by those who have loved her? [51] The wonder-icon itself and legends associated with it is another manifestation of popular piety—indeed an immense subject, touched upon in an earlier study in which we tried to point out ways of approaching it and to draw attention to the contribution of secular literature.

Not only do the portrayals of the Mother of God and saints manifest popular belief and piety, but iconographic changes, often details in compositions, may also be expressions of personal sentiment. Notice, for example, the Dormition icon in the Wijenburgh collection (Pl. XXc). Christ holding the soul of Mary into heaven, breaks the hieratic composition normally found in depictions of the subject, and bends tenderly over His mother as of to bid her farewell. Or notice in the icon of the Forty Martyrs of Sebaste, now in San Diego, how one martyr sustains the other, with what compasion the hands offer the needed support (Pl. XXVIb).

Popular piety can also be manifested through style, as a study of the so-called 'schools of icon painting' can show. The new attitude towards the icon, the icon as a work of art, and the resulting stylistic changes' observed in the last phases of Byzantine art and carried into the Russian schools, correspond to and express inner needs of the believer. The artist, after all, finds ways to express his piety, his spiritual state of being. One has to look, for instance, at the fourteenth-century Crucifixion icon in Athens (Pl. XVIa). The melancholy, sad expression of the Mother of God, standing like a frozen column at the side of the cross, symbol of immense sadness into the depths of which no human being can penetrate for her mantle fences her around, indicates the artist's devotion, his own participation in the Passion. One can also look at a group of icons illustrating the veneration rendered to icons by the faithful who believe that icon painting started with St. Luke. He first painted the portrait of Mary who blessed it and thus sanctified icon painting (Pl. XXXIXa). The triumph of icons was a reaffirmation of this belief. Even saints are venerating icons (Pl. XLa). A believer knows that he can pray to an icon, for at the consecration of an icon the priest asks the Lord: "we beseech you, our king, to send the grace of your holy spirit and your angel to this icon, so that if one prays to it his prayers may be fulfilled ..." [52] In the theme of the Sleep of the Just found on icons, a faithful prays before an icon of Christ for a good sleep, while an archangel writes down the man's good deeds and another one chases Satan away (Pl. XLb). The icon expresses the Christian's hope for healing and health.

The Orthodox Christian believes that the body is sanctified together with the soul and has a great reverance for the holy relics which, like the icons, are channels of divine power. It may be an object associated with the saint, like the *soros* of the Virgin Mary at the Blachernae Church, for example, which had miraculous powers; or it may be the body of a saint, like that of St. Spyridon the patron saint of Corfu, miraculously preserved from corruption (Pl. XLIIa); of primary importance is the relic of the True Cross whose Discovery and Elevation (Church Feast, September 14) have found a place on icons (Pl. XLIb). The veneration of the Cross shows that Orthodoxy is not concerned only with the divine glory of Christ. His humanity and sufferings are not forgotten. The Cross is the symbol

---

[51] See an icon in the Byzantine Museum, Athens, no. 1028, Sotiriou, G., *Guide du Musé byzantin d'Athènes*, A. Chadjinikolaou ed., Athens 1955, p. 31.

[52] Goar, J., Ed., *Euchologion*, Venice 1730, p. 672.

of victory over death and at the same time a manifestation of Christ's outward humilation.

The concern of the faithful for Christ's humanity is further indicated in another group of icons related to the *loca sancta*, the places of the Holy Land where the incarnate Christ lived as a man.[53] Every Christian wishes to experience Christ's life on earth by a pilgrimage to the local sites, as is often stated in texts such as the following from *Pratum spirituale* by Moschus, chapter XCI: "... brother Thalaeleos foresaw his end. And he begged the old man (an anchorite), saying, 'Take me to Jerusalem to worship the Holy Cross and the holy place of the resurrection of Christ our Lord. For during these days the Lord will receive me.' And the old man, taking him, went to the Holy City. And they worshiped the holy and venerable relics..."[54] Icons make the *loca sancta* ever-present (Pls. XLII-XLIV).

Another type of devotion, which may, however, have political and social implications, is expressed in a group of icons which deserve a special study, for they may illuminate what has been termed the secular role of the icon. In an icon made in Mount Athos for the Austrian imperial house, the Emperor Leopold I and his third wife Eleonora Magdalena are depicted as supplicants below the Mother of God shown in half-figure in a water basin with the form of a chalice, a type known as "The Source of Life," a pictorialization of an epithet given to Mary by Joseph the hymnographer in the ninth century (Pl. XLV). At the same time the imperial couple participate in the scheme of the divine economy developed by the icon's supplementary themes. The same concept is pictorialized in another way in the Ushakov icon, in Moscow (Pl. XLVIb). A composition, known as the Tree of Jesse, normally used for a representation of Christ's genealogy has been modified here by placing in the centre the Virgin of Vladimir. On the branches of the tree which rises through the roof of the Dormition Cathedral, Kremlin, are not the ancestors of Christ but the princes of the court and of the Russian Church and the most popular saints. The tree is planted by Ivan Kalita, watered by the Metropolitan Peter and venerated by the members of the new dynasty, the kneeling Tsar Alexei on the left and his wife and sons on the right. Christ spreads His protective mantle over them. Thus the icon represents the family tree of the Moscow rulers in a composition that constitutes an imperial claim and at the same time it glorifies the Mother of God.

Any thorough discussion of the problems of the so-called secular role of the icon should include a large number of icons depicting, for instance, miraculous interventions in the battlefield, the blessings given upon a ruler, an army, a city, by an icon.

Moreover, among didactic subjects, there are some on icons pertaining to the secular aspect of the icon. Their sources must be sought in the folklore tradition of a nation. These icons have a strong moralizing character and are, strictly speaking, popular creations, the best expressions of people's religious sentiments. The theme of the Wheel of Life is well known on Greek icons [55] and so is the paradisal bird Siren on Russian icons, which plays an important role in edifying writings, legends and folklore-poetry (Pl. XXXVIIIb). Similar types of poetry have also provided a text the pictorialization of which represents the snares of the passion of Love. In a Greek icon, dated from 1825, the winged,

---

[53] Weitzmann, K., "*Loca Sancta* and the Representational Arts of Palestine," *Dumbarton Oaks Papers*, 28 (1974), 33-35.

[54] Minge, *PG.*, 87, III, 2949.

[55] See, for example, an icon in the Byzantine Museum, Athens, no. 774, Sotiriou, *op. cit.*, p. 36.

blinded Eros, sitting on top of a column, plays a double trumpet, inviting his victims (Pl. XXXVIIIc). Below a man on the left and a woman on the right, both winged and playing musical instruments, are firmly in the grip of the mouth of dragons. The theme has been identified, not correctly in our opinion, as Eros and the Sirens. In fact the icon contains verses of a folklore song, popular in the island of Siphnos, which fully explain the composition: "(Those given to the passion of love) play and dance and they think that they are flying and that they see and possess all the joys of the world; they do not know that they are in the mouths of beasts." The blind Eros is the seducer and those who yield to his call find themselves without realizing it in the mouths of monsters. The moralizing character of the theme echoes Greek antiquity but the Eros on top of the column stems from the Christian iconography of the pillar saints, the stylites. The composition takes us back to the original purpose of man's making images in general which is that of controllling whatever he fears by means of a representation. In this case the icon painter attempts to influence, to exorcise the power of the passion of love thus exercising a religious function that reveals to us a "magico-religious" aspect of the icon, deeply rooted in the soul of the people.[56] In the long run the icon will expell all evil spirits.

---

[56] Leeuw van der, G., *Sacred and Profane Beauty*, London 1963, pp. 115ff.

CATALOGUE OF ILLUSTRATIONS

The bibliography cited under each item aims at providing the reader with one basic source of information and an adequate illustration. Since these goals are not always met in a single work, it was necessary, in some instances, to cite a second publication.

Plate I a

Bust of Christ Pantocrator.
Byzantine, first half sixth century, Encaustic icon, 84 × 45.5 × 1.2 cm.
Sinai, Monstery of St. Catherine, Gallery.
Lit.: K. Weitzmann, *The Monastery of St. Catherine at Mount Sinai, The Icons*, 1, Princeton, N.J. 1976, no. B. 1, pls. I-II, XXXIX-XLI.

Plate I b

Bust of Christ Pantocrator,
Byzantine, end of fourteenth century. 110 × 66 cm.
Stockholm, National Museum, NM Icon 276.
Lit.: J. Taylor, *Icon Painting*, Oxford 1979, pl. on p. 19; *Byzantine Art an European Art*, Exhibition Catalogue, Athens 1964, no. 202.

Plate I c

Christ the Saviour by Andrey Rublyov
Russian, ca. 1420. 158 × 106 cm.
Fragment from the iconostasis of the Zvenigorod cathedral, near Moscow. Now Moscow, Tretyakov Gallery, inv. no. 12863, cat no. 229.
Lit.: M. V. Antonova, and N. E. Mneva, *Gosudarstvennaia Tret'iakovaskaia gallereia. Katalog drevnerusskoi zhivopisi*, I, Moscow 1963, no. 229, pl. 189; K. Onasch, *Icons*, London 1961, pl. 392, pls. 94, 95.

Plate II a

Christ in Glory and the Twelve Apostles.
Constantinople, fourteenth century. 96 × 78 cm.
Venice, Hellenic Institute, cat. no. 2.
Christ seated on two seraphim is surrounded by the four symbols of the evangelists whose order, read counter clockwise, is that of Epiphanios: Matthew-angel; Mark-lion; Luke-calf; John-eagle.
Lit.: M. Chatzidakis, *Icônes de Saint-Georges des Grecs et de la Collections de l'institut Hellénique de Venise*, Venice 1962, no. 2, pl. I; M. Manoussacas and A. Paliouras, *Guide to the Museum of Icons and the Church of St. George*, Venice 1976, no. 29, pl. IX.

Plate II b

Christ in Glory.

Russian (Moscow), sixteenth century. 74 × 58 cm.

Private Collection.

Christ seated on a throne rests His feet on the fiery wheels beheld by Ezekiel. His throne hovers in a glory containing six-winged seraphs, while the points of a star display the symbols of the evangelists whose identification follows the order of Irenaeus: Matthew-angel; Mark-eagle; Luke-calf; John-lion.

Lit.: E. Dergazarian and M. Van Rijn, *Important Icons from Private Collections*, Exhibition Catalogue, Museum Het Prinsenhof, Delft, Holland, 1977, no. 8.

Plate III a

King Abgarus and the Mandylion (Detail from a triptych).

Byzantine (Palestinian?), mid tenth century. Complete panel about 28 × 9.5 cm.

Sinai, Monastery of St. Catherine, Gallery, glass case.

Lit.: K. Weitzmann, "The Mandylion and Constantine Porphyrogennetos," *Cahiers archéologiques*, 11 (1960), 163-184, fig. 3; Id., *The Monastery of St. Catherine at Mount Sinai, The Icons*, 1, Princeton, N.J. 1976, no. B. 58, *pls.* XXXVI-XXXVII, CXIII-CXV.

Plate III b

The Bringing of the Mandylion by Pervusha.

Russian (Strognanov School), first quarter seventeenth century. 40 × 34 cm.

From the Nikolsky Edinoverchsky Monastery, Moscow. Now Moscow, Tretyakov Gallery, inv. no. 15022, cat. no. 783.

To the left of the panel the painter Ananias displays the Mandylion which cured Abgar, the King of Edessa, who is shown risen from his sick bed to give thanks for his discovery, followed by his subjects. Abgar's palace is set in the background.

Lit.: M. V. Antonova and N. E. Mneva, *Gosudastvennaia Tret'iakovskaia gallereia. Katalog drevnerusskoi zhivopisi*, 2, no. 783, pl. 105; David and Tamara Talbot Rice, *Icons and Their Dating*, London 1974, p. 155, pl. 135.

Plate III c

The Holy Face (The Mandylion).

Russian, seventeenth century. 31.5 × 27 × 3 cm.

Switzerland, Richenthal. Collection Curée J. K. Felber, Pfarrei St. Cäcilia, no. 24.

Lit.: M. Chatzidakis, et al., *Les icones dans les collections suisses*, Berne 1968, no. 170.

Plate IV a

The Hospitality of Abraham.

Byzantine (Constantinople), end fourteenth century. 33 × 60 cm.

Athens, Benaki Museum, cat. no. 2.

Lit.: M. Chatzidakis, "Ikonen aus Griechenland," in K. Weitzmann et al., *Die Ikonen*, Herrsching-Ammersee 1977, pp. 82, 106, pl. 110.

Plate IV b

Paternity.
Russian (Yaroslav?), end sixteenth century. 105.2 × 72.7 cm.
London, Temple Gallery.
The icon represents God the Father, Christ Emmanuel and the Holy Ghost, within a lozenge-shaped glory of light, seated on a throne surrounded by cherubim and seraphim contained in an oval-shaped glory, set on a star on the four point of which are the symbols of the evangelists.
Lit.: Temple Gallery, *Masterpieces of Byzantine and Russian Icon Painting*, Exhibition Catalogue, London 1974, no. 29.

Plate IV c

The Holy Trinity.
Greek (Crete), second half sixteenth century. 44 × 35 cm.
Private Collection.
Lit.: E. Dergazarian and M. Van Rijn, *Important Icons from Private Collections*, Exhibition Catalogue, Amsterdam 1976, no. 10.

Plate V a

Mother of God "Hodegetria".
Byzantine, first half thirteenth century. Mosaic-icon, 80 × 84 cm.
From a destroyed church of Calatamauro, near Entella, Sicily.
Palermo, Galleria Regionale di Palazzo Abatellis, inv. no. 2.
Lit.: V. Lazarev. *Storia della pittura bizantina*, Turin 1967, fig. 417; R. Delogi, *La Galleria Nationale della Sicilia*, Rome 1962, pp. 24, 58.

Plate V b

Mother of God "Galaktotrophousa".
Greek, end seventeenth century. 28 × 21 cm.
Athens, Benaki Mseum, inv. no. 3026, cat. no. 55.
Lit.: A. Xyngopoulos, *Katalogos ton eikonon tou mouseiou Benaki*, Athens 1936, no. 55, pl. 40b.

Plate V c

Mother of God of Don (Donskaja) by Theophanes the Greek.
Russian, 1392. 86 × 68 cm.
Moscow, Tretyakov Gallery, inv. no. 14244, cat. no. 216.
Lit.: M. V. Antonova and N. E. Mneva, *Gosudarstvennaia Tret'iakovaskaia gallereia Katalog drevnerusskoi zhivopisi*, 2, Moscow 1963, no. 216, pl. 173.

Plate VI a

Mother of God "The Symbols of the Passion" attributed to Nicolas Ritzos (?).
Creto-Venetian, last quarter fifteenth century. 91 × 77 cm.
Princeton, N. J., The Art Museum, Princeton University. Acc. no. 33.

Lit.: T. Gouma Peterson, "Crete, Venice, the 'Madonneri' and a Creto-Venetian Icon in the Allen Art Museum," *Allen Memorial Art Museum Bulletim*, 25 (1968), 53-86, fig. 4.

Plate VI b

Mother of God "Blachernitissa".
Byzantine, twelfth century. Marble, 76 × 136 cm.
Venice, Church S. Maria Mater Domini.
Lit.: R. Lange, *Die byzantinische Reliefikone*, Recklinghausen 1964, no. 6. Photo, Oswald Böhm, Venice.

Plate VI c

Mother of God of the Sign (Źnamenje).
Russian (Novgorod), early sixteenth century. Bilateral, processional icon. 75 × 54 cm. without holder, 111 × 54 cm with holder, see Pl. Xb.
Holland, Echteld. Collection Kasteel "De Wijenburgh," no. 7104.
Lit.: Hetty, J. Roozemond van Ginhoven, *Ikon, Kunst-Geist und Glaube*, Exhibition Catalogue, Recklinghausen and Echteld 1980, no. 33.

Plate VII a

The Virgin Orans.
Byzantine, 1235-1261. 28 × 22 cm. with frame.
Freising, Cathedral, on silver altar by Hans Krumper and Gottfried Land, 1629.
On the metal frame, with silver gilt covering, rectangular plates with Greek inscriptions alternate with enamel medallions containing the Hetoimasia and two archangels on top; below, horizontally read: Peter and Paul, George and Demetrius; bottom, Cosmas and Damian, last medallion on the right is missing. The pose of the Virgin is that known as the "Hagiosoritissa," The dedicatory inscription mentions a Manuel Disykatos, bishop of Thessalonike between 1235 and 1261.
Lit.: David and Tamara Talbot Rice, *Icons and Their Datings*, London 1974, p. 27, pl. 6; S. Benker and P. Steiner, *Diözesan Museum Freising*, (Bildheft, 1), 2nd ed., Munich-Zurich 1977, fig. on pp. 22, 24.

Plate VII b

Mother of God Enthroned, Apostles and 'Majestas Domini'.
Egypt, sixth-seventh century. Tapestry weave hanging, 179 × 100 cm.
Cleveland, Ohio. The Cleveland Museum of Art, CMA 67. 144, Purchase, the Leonard "C. Hanna Jr., Bequest Fund."
Lit.: K. Weitzmann, *The Icon*, N. York 1978, no. 4; Shepherd, D., "An Icon of the Virgin. A Sixth Century Tapestry Panel from Egypt," *Bulletin of the Cleveland Museum of Art*, March 1969, pp. 90[ff].

Plate VIII

The Sacrifice of Abraham.
Greek, nineteenth century. 115 × 73 cm.
Athens, Byzantine Museum, cat. no. 751.

The icon depicts the departure of Abraham and Isaac from their home, below; the sacrifice at the top and their safe return in the centre.

Lit.: J. Taylor, *Icon Painting*, London 1979, pl. on pp. 62, 63.

Plate IX a

The Three Hebrews in the Fiery Furnace.

Byzantine (Palestine), about seventh century. Encaustic icon, 35.5 × 49.6 × 1.1 cm. Sinai, Monastery of St. Catherine. Gallery, glass case.

Lit.: K. Weitzmann, *The Monastery of St. Catherine at Mount Sinai, The Icons*, 1, Princeton 1976, no. B. 31, pls. XXII and LXXXII-LXXXIII.

Plate IX b

The Three Hebrews in the Fiery Furnace.

Russian (Novgorod), about 1500. A bilateral 'Tabletka,' 24.5 × 20 cm., see Pl. XXVIb. San Diego, Calif., The Timken Art Gallery. Formerly Echteld, Coll. Kasteel "De Wijenburgh".

The icon shows the three Hebrews in the fire being comforted by an angel while to the right the king Nebuchadnezzär and his attendants witness the miracle (Daniel, 3).

Lit.: H. Skrobucha, *Bongers Ikonenkalender* 1979, Recklinghausen 1979; Temple Gallery, *Byzantine, Greek and Russian Icons*, Exhibition catalogue, London 1979, no 23.

Photo, Kasteel "De Wijenburgh".

Plate IX c

The Prophet Daniel in the Lions' Den.

Byzantine (Constantinople), fourteenth century. 28 × 23 cm.

Athens, Byzantine Museum, cat. no. 1556.

Daniel praying in the lions' den is nourished by Habakkuk, depicted to the right, brought miraculously by an angel.

Lit.: J. Taylor, *Icon Painting*, Oxford 1979, fig. on p. 39.

Plate X a

The Prophet Elijah.

Byzantine (Constantinople), end twelftth century. 130 × 70 cm.

Sinai, Monastery of St. Catherine.

Lit.: Georges and Maria Sotiriou, *Icônes du Mont Sinai*, 1 (Plates), 2 (Text), Athens 1956, 1958, pl. 74, p. 88; K. Weitzmann, "The Classical in Byzantine Art as a Mode of Individual Expression," *Byzantine Art an European Art*, Lectures, Athens 1966, pp. 150-177.

Plate X b

The Ascension of Elijah; on the borders St. Nicholas of Myra and Basil the Great.

Russian (Novgorod), early sixteenth century. Bilateral, processional icon, reverse of Pl. VIc. 57 × 54 cm. without holder, 111 × 54 cm. with holder.

Holland, Echteld. Collection Kasteel "De Wijenburgh," no. 7104.

The prophet is taken up into heaven in a chariot of fire (II Kings 2:8-15). At the moment of his departure he drops his mantle to Elisha, his disciple.

Lit.: See Pl. VIc.

Plate X c

The Ascension of Elijah.
Greek (Northern Greece), second half seventeenth century. 86 × 63 cm.
Athens, National Gallery, inv. no. 4952.
Lit.: Unpublished.

Plate XI

Great Deesis and Dodekaorton, Triptych.
Greek (Venice), reign Pope Paul III (1534-1549), about 1540-1549. Central panel
127 × 106.2 cm; left wing 119. 9 × 49.5 cm; right wing 119 × 49. 5 cm.
U.S.A., Madison, Wisconsin. The Elvehjem Art Museum, acc. no. 37. 1.1, gift Joseph
E. Davies, cat. no. 1.
Christ as the Great Archpriest is flanked by Mary and John the Baptist; officiating
angels, left and right above. Beneath the feet of Christ, there is the coat of arms of Pope
Paul III. The twelve Great Feasts are represented on the wings as follows, beginning from
the left: Annunciation, Nativity, Presentation of Christ to the Temple, Baptism, Entry
into Jerusalem, Resurrection of Lazarus, Pentecost, Ascension, Crucifixion, Dormition,
Anastasis, Transfiguration.
Lit.: G. Galavaris, *Icons from the Elvehjem Art Center*, The University of Wisconsin,
Madison 1973, no. 1.

Plate XII a

The Twelve Feasts (Originally part of a quadriptych).
Byzantine (Constantinople), early twelfth century. 65 × 46 × 3 cm.
Sinai, Monastery of St. Catherine, Bema, iconostasis.
Lit.: K. Weitzmann, "The Cycle of the Great Feasts," New Grecian Gallery, *Feasts Day
Icons*, Exhibition catalogue, London 1973, fig. 3.

Plate XII b

The "Ustyug" Annunciation.
Russian (Novgorod), probably between 1119-1130. 229 × 144 cm.
From the Dormition Cathedral, Moscow. Now Moscow, Tretyakov Gallery, inv. no.
25539, cat. no. 4.
Lit.: M. V. Antonova and N. E. Mneva, *Gosudarstvennaia Tret'iakovskaia gallereia.
Katalog drevnerusskoi zhivopisi*, I, Moscow 1963, no. 4, pl. 20; K. Onasch, *Icons*, London
1961, p. 354, pls. 15, 16; David and Tamara Talbot Rice, *Icons and Their Dating*, London
1974, pl. 174.

Plate XII c

The Annunciation, Iconostasis Doors.
Byzantine, second half fifteenth century. Each leaf 119.5 × 32.3 × 1.9 cm.
Sinai, Monastery of St. Catherine. Chapel Hagioi Pente Martyres.
Lit.: Unpublished.
Photo Papachatzidakis, Photographic Archive, Benaki Museum, Athens.

Plate XIII a

The Annunciation.
Byzantine (Constantinople), end of twelfth century. About 57 × 42 cm.
Sinai, Monastery of St. Catherine, installed in the seventeenth century iconostasis.
Lit.: K. Weitzmann et al., *Die Ikonen*, Herrsching-Ammersee 1977, pp. 27, 60, 222, 236,
pl. 54.

Plate XIII b

The Annunciation.
Russian (Jaroslav), seventeenth century. 31 × 28 cm.
Holland, Echteld. Collection Kasteel "De Wijenburgh", no. 4141.
Lit.: H. Skrobucha, *Bongers Ikonenkalender 1979*, Recklinghausen 1979.

Plate XIV

The Birth and Infancy of Christ.
Byzantine, twelfth century. 36.3 × 21.2 cm.
Siani, Monastery of St. Catherine.
The Birth of Christ is flanked by the Journey and the Adoration of the Magi(left),
the Annunciation to the Shepherds and the Departure of the Magi (right), the Doxology
of the Angels (above) and the Bathing of the Child (below). The lower half depicts the
Dream of Joseph, the Flight into and the Arrival in Egypt (a son of Joseph from an earlier
marriage is added to the scene); the Flight of Elizabeth with the infant John in a cave;
and the Massacre of the Innocents.
Lit.: K. Weitzmann et al., *Die Ikonen*, Herrsching-Ammersee 1977, pp. 41, 221, pls. 44,
45

Plate XV a

The Baptism of Christ.
Byzantine, end fourteenth century. 50.5 × 37 cm.
Jerusalem, Greek Patriarchate, Chapel of St. Thecla, no. 43.
Lit.: M. Chatzidakis, "Ikonen aus Griechenland" in K. Weitzmann et al., *Die Ikonen*,
Herrsching-Ammersee 1977, pp. 82, 135, 226, 238, pl. 113.
Photo, Dr. M. Chatzidakis.

Plate XV b

The Baptism of Christ.
Byzantine, mid fourteenth century. 40 × 32 cm.
Belgrade, National Museum, no. 4348.
Lit.: S. Radojčič, "Ikonen aus Jugoslawien" in K. Weitzmann et al., *Die Ikonen*,
Herrsching-Ammersee 1977, pp. 151, 239-240, pl. 153.

Plate XV c

The Raising of Lazarus.
Byzantine, second half fifteenth century. 45 × 32 cm.
Oxford Ashmolean Museum, cat. no. 40.

Lit.: D. Talbot Rice, *Art of the Byzantine Era*, London 1963, pp. 262, 263, pl. 247; *Byzantine Art an European Art*, Catalogue 9th Exhibition Council of Europe, 2nd ed., Athens 1964, no. 181.

Plate XVI a

The Crucifixion.
Byzantine (Constantinople), fourteenth century, Bilateral icon, 103 × 84 cm.
Athens, Byzantine Museum, cat. no. 169.
Lit.: M. Chatzidakis, "Ikonen aus Griechenland" in K. Weitzmann, et al., *Die Ikonen*, Herrsching-Ammersee 1977, pp. 78, 224, pl. 79.

Plate XVI b

The Crucifixion by Andreas Pavias.
Creto-Venetian, end fifteenth century. 83.5 × 59 cm.
Athens, National Gallery, inv. no. 144.
Lit.: A. Xyngopoulos, *Schediasma tes threskeutikes zographikes meta ten alosin*, Athens 1957, pp. 173^ff, pl. 48. 2.

Plate XVI c

The Descent from the Cross.
Greek (Crete), seventeenth century. 38 × 27 cm.
Athens, Benaki Museum, inv. no. 3729.
Lit: M. Chatzidakis, "He Kretike zographike kai he italike chalkographia," *Kretika Chronika*, 10 (1947), 27-47, pl. Z.2.

Plate XVII a

The Three Marys at the Tomb of Christ and the Appearance of Christ to Them.
Russian (Moscow), late sixteenth century. 31.7 × 27.3 cm.
Formerly in Hann Collection, U.S.A.
Lit.: Tamara Talbot Rice, *Russian Icons*, N. York 1963, pl. XLII.

Plate XVII b

The "Chairete," Christ's Appearence to the Virgin Mary and Mary Magdalene, attributed to Theophanes the Cretan, 1546. 56 × 40 cm.
Athos, Monastery of Stavroniketa, iconostasis.
Lit.: A. Karakatsani, "Oi eikones tes mones Stavroniketa," in *Mone Stavroniketa*, Athens (National Bank of Greece) 1974, no. 15, pl. 25. Photo, National Bank of Greece, courtesy of the Monastery.

Plate XVIII

Christ's Descent into Hell.
Byzantine, fourteenth-fifteenth century. 47 × 62 cm.
Venice, Hellenic Institute, acc. no. 7.
Lit.: M. Chatzidakis, *Icônes de Saint-Georges des Grecs et de la collection de l'institut Hellénique de Venise*, Venise 1962, no. 11. pl. IV; M. Manoussacas and A. Paliouras, *Guide to the Museum of Icons and the Church of St. George*, Venice 1976, no. 38, pl. XIII.

Plate XIX a

Christ's Descent into Hell, Eastern Icon (Detail).

Russian (Moscow), first half seventeenth century. 35.5 × 30 cm.

Berlin, Staatlichen Museen Preusischer Kulturbesitz; Früchristlich-Byzantinischer Sammlung, inv. no. 9637.

Lit.: V. H. Elbern, *Ikonen aus der Frühchristlich-Byzantinischer Sammlung, Staatliche Museen Preussischer Kulturbesitz*, Berlin 1970, no. 21.

Photo, Jörg P. Anders, West Berlin.

Plate XIX b

The Ascension.

Russian (Vologda?), end fifteenth century. 60 × 46 cm.

Holland, Echteld. Collection Kasteel "De Wijenburgh" no. 6006.

Lit.: B. Velthuis, R. Roozemond, V. Gerrtsen-Sawwik, *Ikon-Maria*, Echteld 1979, no. 63.

Plate XIX c

Pentecost.

Greek, early eighteenth century.

Mount Athos, Karyai. Cell Dionysius of Fourna.

Lit.: Unpublished.

Photo, Papachatzidakis, Photographic Archive, Benaki Museum, Athens.

Plate XX a

The Dormition of the Mother of God by Theophanes the Greek.

Russian, about 1392. 86 × 68 cm., the reverse of a bilateral icon. Formerly in the Dormition Cathedral at Kolomna. Moscow, Tretyakov Gallery, cat. no. 216.

According to the Apocrypha the candle burning before the bier was lit by Mary herself when an angel informed her that her death was imminent.

Lit.: H. P. Gerhard, *Die Welt der Ikonen*, 3rd ed., Recklinghausen 1970, p. 152, fig.47; V. N. Lazarev, *Feofan Grek i ego shkola*, Moscow 1961, pp. 63-67.

Plate XX b

The Dormition of the Mother of God.

Russian (Moscow), first half seventeenth century. 31 × 27.5 cm.

Vienna, Kunsthistorisches Museum, Sammlung für Plastik und Kunstgewerbe, inv. no. 234.

Lit.: K. Kreidl-Papadopoulos, "Die Ikonen im Kunsthistorischen Museum in Wien," *Jahrbuch der Kunsthistorischen Sammlungen in Wien*, 66, n.S. 30 (1970), 49-144, no. 17, pl. 106.

Plate XX c

The Dormition of the Mother of God.

Russian (Pskov), second half sixteenth century. 35.5 × 31 × 3 cm.

Holland, Echteld. Collection Kasteel "De Wijenburgh," no. 5166.

Lit.: M. Lazović, *Icones d'une Collection Privée, Musée d'art et d'Histoire*, Geneva 1974, no. 8.

Plate XXI a

The Archangel Gabriel.
Cyprus, 1544. 83 × 69.5 cm.
Cyprus, Monastery of St. Neophytos. From a Great Deesis in the iconostasis of the Catholicon.
Lit.: A. Papageorgiou, *Ikonen aus Zypern*, Munich, Geneva, Paris 1969, p. 118, pl. 81.
Photo, Dept. of Antiquities, Nicosia, Cyprus.

Plate XXI b

The Archangel Michael and Donor.
Byzantine, end twelfth century. 42 × 28 cm.
Sinai, Monastery of St. Catherine.
Lit.: Georges and Maria Sotiriou, *Icônes du Mont Sinai*, 1 (Plates), 2 (Text), Athens 1956, 1958, p. 139, pl. 159.
Photo, Papachatzidakis, Photographic Archives Benaki Museum, Athens.

Plate XXI c

The Miracle at Chonai.
Byzantine (Constantinople), mid fourteenth century, 42.5 × 35.6 cm.
Jerusalem, Greek Patriarchate.
Lit.: M. Chatzidakis, "Iconen aus Griechenland" in K. Weitzmann, et al., *Die Ikonen*, Herrsching-Ammersee 1977, pp. 78, 226, pl. 106 Photo. Dr. M. Chazidakis.

Plate XXI d

The Archangel Michael Overcomes Satan.
Russian, late sixteenth century. 57 × 45 cm.
Switserland, Kölliken. Collection Dr. S. Amberg-Herzog, no. 152b.
Lit.: *Kunst der Ostkirche*, Stift Herzogenburg. Exhibition Catalogue, Vienna 1977, no. 154, pl. 73.

Plate XXII a

St. John the Baptist.
Byzantine (Constantinople), third quarter fourteenth century. 41 × 31. 5 cm.
Holland, Amsterdam. Collection Michel Van Rijn.
Lit.: E. Degazarian and M. Van Rijn, *Important Icons from Private Collections*, Exhibition Catalogue, Amsterdam 1976, no. 53.

Plate XXII b

The Apostle Peter by the Priest Euphrosynos.
Greek (Crete), 1542. 114 × 84 cm.
Mount Athos, Monastery of Dionysiou.
Lit.: M. Chatzidakis, "Ho zographos Euphrosynos," *Kretika Chronika*, 10 (1956), 273-291, pl. KZ.
Photo, Dr. M. Chatzidakis.

Plate XXII c

The Apostle Paul.
Cyprus, thirteenth century. 94 × 67 cm.
Cyprus, Nicosia. Church of the Virgin Chrysaliniotissa.
Lit.: A. Papageorgiou, *Icons from Cyprus*, Benaki Museum, Exhibition Catalogue,
Athens 1976, no. 16.
Photo, Dept. of Antiquities, Nicosia, Cyprus.

Plate XXIII a

The Ecstatic Meeting of Peter and Paul.
Greek (Crete), end of sixteenth century. 41.5 × 2.5 cm.
Patmos, Monastery of St. John Theologian, New Treasury.
Lit.: M. Chatzidakis, *Eikones tes Patmou*, Athens 1977, no. 74, pp. 124, 125, pl. 45.
Photo, National Bank of Greece, Courtesy of the Monastery.

Plate XXIII b

Peter and Paul Holding the Church.
Greek, end of sixteenth century.
Mount Athos, Monastery of Iveron.
Lit.: Unpublished. Photo Papachatzidakis, Photographic Archive Benaki Museum.
Athens.

Plate XXIII c

St. Nicholas of Myra.
Byzantine, tenth-eleventh century (frame early thirteenth). Mosaic, silver and precious
stones. Complete panel with frame 31 × 25 cm. Aachen, Pharrkirche St. Johan-B.
The mosaic is set in a silver gilt frame decorated with precious stones and repoussé
representations of the symbols of the evangelists, St. Gregory and St. Benedict and episodes
from the life of St. Nicholas.
Lit.: *Byzantine Art an European Art*, Exhibition catalogue, Athens 1964, no. 161.
Photo, Dr. Hans Michael Franke, Grashofweg Str., Ratingen.

Plate XXIV

St. John "Chrysostom 'Fountain of Wisdom'".
Byzantine (Constantinople), last quarter of thirteenth century. 40.5 × 31.5 cm.
Athens, Lomberdo Museum, no. 248.
The central part of the icon represents St. John Chrysostom receiving inspiration from
Paul and transmitting his wisdom to his listeners; on the upper part Moses on the left and
Peter with John on the right confirm the transmission of divine wisdom. On the frame,
upper centre, there is the Hetoimasia and left and right, horizontally read, one sees the
following saints: Peter-Paul; Luke-John; Mark-Matthew; Andrew-Simon; Onuphrios-
Anthony-Panteleimon, Nicholas of Myra, Basil the Great, John Chrysostom, Gregory
Nazianzenus, John the Baptist.
Lit.: A. Xyngopoulos, "Aghios Ioannes hos Chrysostomos 'Pege Sophias'," *Archaeologike
Ephemeris*, (1942-1944), 1948, 1-36, pl. 1.

Plate XXV a

St. Demetrius.
Byzantine (Yugoslavia), end of fourteenth, beginning fifteenth century. 34.5 × 26.5 cm.
Belgrade, Museum of Applied Arts.
Lit.: S. Radojčić, "Ikonen aus Jugoslawien," in K. Weitzmann, et al., *Die Ikonen*,
Herrsching-Ammersee 1977, pp. 154, 232, pl. 191.

Plate XXV b

St. George.
Byzantine, fourteenth-fifteenth century. Painted wood, 19 × 15.5 cm.
Athens, Benaki Museum, inv. no. 2974, cat. no. 3.
Lit.: A. Xyngopoulos, *Katalogos ton eikonon tou Mouseiou Benaki*, Athens 1936, no. 3,
pl. 6.

Plate XXV c

St. George and the Dragon.
Russian (Novgorod), late fifteenth century. 40.6 × 33.3 cm.
Formerly Hann Collection, U.S.A.
Lit.: Tamara Talbot Rice, *Russian Icons*, N. York 1963, pl. XXVI.

Plate XXV d

St. George and the Dragon.
Russian (Moscow) about 1600. 38.5 × 31.5 × 1.7 cm.
Private Collection.
Lit.: Unpublished.

Plate XXVI a

Saints from September to November, Calendar Icon.
Byzantine, eleventh century. 55 × 45 × 0.15 cm.
Sinai, Monastery of St. Catherine.
Lit.: K. Weitzmann, "Byzantine Miniature and Icon Painting in the Eleventh Century,"
Proceedings of the XIIIth Inter. Congress of Byzantine Studies, Oxford 1966, London 1967,
209-224, pl. 35.

Plate XXVI b

The Forty Martyrs of Sebaste.
Russian (Novgorod), about 1500. Reverse side of 'Tabletka' Pl. IXb, 24.5 × 20 cm.
San Diego, Calif., The Timken Art Gallery. Formerly Echteld, Coll. Kasteel "De Wijen-
burgh."
Lit.: See Pl. IXb. Photo, Echteld, Kasteel "De Wijenburgh".

Plate XXVI c

The Martyrdom of St. Charalampes.
Greek, end eighteenth century. Painted on an alms box, panel 22.8 × 16 × 1.7 cm, box
22.8 × 17 × 13.2 cm.
Toronto, The Royal Ontario Museum, ROM 948.1.107.

The hieromartyr Charalampes, commemorated by the Orthodox Church on February 10, was a priest in Magnesia (Lydia) and suffered martyrdom under the emperor Severus (193-211). Galena, the emperor's daughter made an effort to save his life, and the painter has probably included her in the group of figures following the executioner. The inscription on the scroll, an invocation of the person who dedicated the alms box, reads in translation: "Lord guard those who perform a memorial service for my sake."

Lit.: Unpublished.

Plate XXVII a

St. Christopher the Cynocephalos (The Dog-headed).
Greek (Asia Minor), seventeenth century. 68 × 36 cm.
Athens, Byzantine Museum, cat. no. 798.
Lit.: G. Sotiriou, *Guide du Musée byzantin d'Athènes*, ed. Chatdjinikolaou, Athens 1955, p. 36, pl. XXXII.

Plate XXVII b

Christ with Sts. Alexandra and Agatha.
Russian (Moscow), seventeenth century. 32.4 × 27 cm.
Ottawa, The National Gallery of Canada, no. 15825.
Lit.: G. Galavaris, "'Christ with Saints Alexandra and Agatha'. A Russian Icon in the National Gallery of Canada," *Bulletin The National Gallery of Canada*, 26 (1975), 24-38.

Plate XXVII c

St. Nicholas of Mozahjsk, Triptychon.
Russian, end sixteenth century. Painted wood, 49 × 41 cm (closed).
Holland, Echteld. Collection Kasteel "De Wijenburgh," no. 3939.
Lit.: Hetty, J. Roozemond van Ginhoven, *Ikon, Kunst-Geist und Glaube*, Exhibition catalogue, Recklinghausen and Echteld 1980, no. 64.

Plate XXVIII a

Christ with abt Menas.
Coptic (from Bawit), sixth-seventh century. Encaustic icon, 57 × 57 × 2.0 cm.
Paris, Musée du Louvre, Dept. des Antiquités chrétiennes, inv. no. X5178.
Lit.: *Koptische Kunst, Christentum am Nil*, Exhibition catalogue, Villa Hügel-Essen 1963, no. 236, color plate IV.

Plate XXVIII b

Sts. Sava and Simeon of Serbia.
Serbian, first half fifteenth century. 32.5 × 26 × 2 cm.
Belgrade, National Museum.
Lit.: S. Radojčić, "Ikonen aus Jugoslavien," in K. Weitzmann, et al., *Die Ikonen*, Herrsching-Ammersee 1977, pp. 154, 217, 241, pl. 185.

Plate XXVIII c

Sts. Sabas and Euthymius.
Greek (Central Greece), fifteenth century. 23.5 × 17 cm.

Holland, Amsterdam. Collection Michel van Rijn.
Lit.: E. Dergazarian and M. Van Rijn, *Important Icons from Private Collections*, Exhibition Catalogue, Museum Het Prinsenhof, Delft, Holland, 1977, no. 73.

Plate XXIX a

St. Onuphrios.
Greek (Greek islands), eighteenth century. 17.2 × 14.2 × 2 cm.
Switzerland, Zumikon. Collection Ing. Hans Bibus.
Lit.: M. Chatzidakis, et al., *Les icones dans les collections suisses*, Berne 1968, no. 55.

Plate XXIX b

St. Simeon the Stylite, the Elder.
Greek (Greek islands), ca. 1700. 42.5 × 31.5 × 2.3 cm.
Switzerland, Kölliken. Collection Dr. S. Amberg-Herzog, A.S./244.
Lit.: M. Chatzidakis, et al., *Les icones dans les collections suisses*, Berne 1968, no. 49.

Plate XXIX c

St. Basil the Great and Basil the Blessed.
Russian (Moscow), ca. 1650-1700. 31.2 × 26.7 cm.
U.S.A., Madison, Wisconsin. The Elvehjem Art Museum, acc. no. 37.1.15, cat. no. 17.
Lit.: G. Galavaris, *Icons from the Elvehjem Art Center*, The University of Wisconsin, Madison, 1973, no. 17.

Plate XXX a

The Heavenly Ladder.
Byzantine, second half twelfth century. 41 × 29.3 cm.
Sinai, The Monastery of St. Catherine.
Lit.: K. Weitzmann, *The Icon*, N. York 1978, pp. 36, 88, pl. 25..

Plate XXX b

The Death of Ephraim the Syrian by Andreas Pavias.
Creto-Venetian, end fifteenth century. 39.5 × 59 cm.
Jerusalem, Greek Patriarchate. Church of St. Constantine, inv. no. 154.
Lit.: *Byzantine art, an European Art*, 9th Exhibition of the Council of Europe, 2nd ed , Athens 1964, no. 266.
Photo, Byzantine Museum, Athens.

Plate XXXI

The Transfiguration and the Forty Raithou Martyrs by George Klonza.
Greek, 1603. 62 × 39 cm.
Sinai, Monastery of St. Catherine. Chapel of the Fathers of Sinai.
Lit.: A. Xyngopoulos, *Schediasma tes threskeutikes zographikes meta ten alosin*, Athens 1957, pp. 174[ff], pl. 47.2; colour plate in National Bank of Greece, *Calendar 1967*.

Plate XXXII

The Annunciation, The Communion of the Apostles, the Four Evangelists, Iconostasis Doors,

Russian (Novgorod), fifteenth century; left leaf 163 × 45 cm, right leaf 164 × 47 cm.
Moscow, Tretyakov Gallery, inv. no. 28649, 28650, cat. no. 53.

Lit.: M. N. Antonova and N. E. Mneva, *Gosudarstvennaia Tret'iakovskaia gallereia. Katalog drevnerusskoi zhivopisi*, 1, Moscow 1963, no. 53, pl. 67.

Plate XXXIII a

Great Deesis; the Virgin, Archangels, Prophets, Apostles and Saints.
Venetian, early fourteenth century. 66 × 137 cm.
Venice, Hellenic Institute, acc. no. 1, cat. no. 178.

Lit.: M. Chatzidakis, *Icônes de Saint-Georges des Grecs et de la Collection de l'institute Hellénique de Venise*, Venice 1962, no. 178; M. Manoussacas and A. Paliouras *Guide to the Museum of Icons and the Church of St. George*, Venice 1976, no. 4, pl. II.

Plate XXXIII b

The Holy Face (The Mandylion).
Russian (Vladimir-Suzdal ?), mid twelfth century. Obverse of double-faced icon (see next plate), 77 × 71 cm.
From the Dormition Cathedral, Moscow. Moscow, Tretyakov Gallery, inv. no. 14245, cat. no. 7.

Lit.: State Tretyakov Gallery, *Early Russian Art*, Moscow 1968, pl. 6; K. Onasch, *Icons*, London 1961, pls. 10, 11.

Plate XXXIII c

The Adoration of the Cross.
Russian (Novgorod), about 1199, 77 × 71 cm., reverse side of above icon.
The two sides of the icon were not painted at the same time or at the same place.
Lit.: See Pl. XXXIIIb.

Plate.: XXXIV a

The Lamentation.
Greek (Crete), about 1500. 44.5 × 49.3 × 2.5 cm.
Patmos, Monastery St. John Theologian. Kathisma Evangelismou, Treasury.
Lit.: M. Chatzidakis, *Eikones tes Patmou*, Athens 1977, no. 21, pl. 21.
Photo, National Bank of Greece, Courtesy of the Monastery.

Plate XXXIV b

Christ the "Vine".
Greek, seventeenth century. 39 × 30 cm.
Athens, Byzantine Museum, cat. no. 1524.
Lit.: G. Sotiriou, *Guide du Musée byzantin d'Athènes*, ed. A. Chadjinikolaou, Athens 1955, p. 17, pl. XXXI.

Plate XXXIV c

Christ the "Vine".
Rumanian, nineteenth century. Painted on glass, 42.5 × 37 cm (without frame).
Recklinghausen, Ikonen-Museum, inv. no. 821.
Lit.: H. Skrobucha, *Kunstsammlungen der Stadt Recklinghausen, Ikonen-Museum*, Catalogue, 4th ed., Recklinghausen 1968, no. 427.

Plate XXXV a

Christ "Image of Pity" (Basileus tes Doxes).
Byzantine, early fourteenth century. Mosaic-icon, 23 × 28 cm with frame, 13 × 19 cm
without frame.
Rome, Church S. Croce in Gerusaleme.
Lit.: C. Bertelli, "The 'Image of Pity' in Santa Croce in Gerusaleme," *Essays in the
History of Art Presented to Rudolf Wittkower*, ed. D. Fraser, London 1967, pp. 40-55, figs 1-4.

Plate XXXV b

Christ, "Image of Pity-The Bread of Life".
Greek, sixteenth-seventeenth century (before 1603). 20.2 × 15.4 × 1.6 cm.
Sinai, Monastery of St. Catherine. Chapel of the Burning Bush.
Lit.: Unpublished.

Plate XXXV c

Mary of Egypt Receiving Communion from Zosimas by Emmanuel Lambardos (?).
Greek (Grete), 1603 (?). 45.3 × 38.2 cm.
U.S.A., Providence, Rhode Island. Museum of Art, Rhode Island School of Design;
Museum Appropriation acc. no. 17.516.
Lit.: Unpublished.

Plate XXXVI

The Divine Liturgy by Joseph (?)
Greek (Ionian islands), eighteenth century. 61 × 50.5 × 2.2 cm.
Toronto, the Royal Ontario Museum, cat. no. 979 × 4.42.
The Holy Trinity represented in the centre is surrounded by the heavenly host. The
open codex on the "altar" contains the blessing of the Litany of Peace which marks the
beginning of the Liturgy. The Great Entrance with the Holy Gifts is shown on the upper
part—the "undefiled" body of the King of Glory is excorted by the angelic hosts for the
sacrifice. The Great Entrance leads to the Eucharistic Anaphora in which Christ officiates:
"thousand of archangels... myriads of angels, the cherubim and seraphim, with six
wings and many eyes soaring aloft: singing, crying, proclaiming the hymn of Victory and
saying: Holy, Holy, Holy, Lord Sabaoth ...".
Lit.: Unpublished.

Plate XXXVII a

The Sacrament of Confession.
Greek (Islands), nineteenth century. 67 × 51 cm.
Athens, Byzantine Museum, cat. no. 754.
The icon represents the purification of the sinner through the sacrament of Confession.
Above, the heavens "rejoice" for the return of the sinner to Paradise and below one sees the
hell with the punishements of the sinners. The confession takes place in front of an icon.
Lit.: Musée Byzantin Athénes, *Icones* (Editions Apollo), N. York 1967, p. 64, no. 2.

Plate XXXVII b

The Sacrament of Confession.
Greek, mid eighteenth century. 24.7 × 21.7 cm.
Vienna, Private Collection.
Lit.: G. Egger, *Späte griechische Ikonen*, Exhibition Catalogue, Österr. Museum für angewandte Kunst, Vienna 1970, no. 54; *Kunst der Ostkirche*, Stift Herzogenburg, Exhibition Catalogue, Vienna 1977, no. 97.
Photo, Österreichisches Museum für angewandte Kunst.

Plate XXXVIII a

The Glorification of the Pure Soul.
Russian (Moscow), beginning seventeenth century. 31 × 27.3 cm.
Vienna, Kunsthistorisches Museum, Collection für Plastik und Kunstgewerbe, inv. no. 233.
Lit.: K. Kreidl-Papadopoulos, "Die Ikonen im Kunsthistorischen Museum in Wien," *Jahrbuch der Kunsthistorischen Sammlungen in Wien*, 66 (1970), no. 16, fig. 55.

Plate XXXVIII b

The Paradisian Bird Siren.
Russian, mid eighteenth century. 44 × 34.8 cm.
Recklinghausen, Ikonen-Museum, inv. no. 895, cat. no. 254.
Lit.: H. Skrobucha, *Kunstsammlungen der Stadt Recklinghausen, Ikonen-Museum*, Catalogue, 4th ed., Recklinghausen 1968, no. 254.

Plate XXXVIII c

Allegory of the Passion of Love by Deutereuon Siphnou.
Greek (Siphnos), November 7, 1825. 67 × 51 cm.
Athens, Byzantine Museum, cat. no. 773.
Lit.: M. Andronikos, M. Chatzidakis, V. Karagiorgis, *Ta Hellenika Mouseia*, Athens 1974, pp. 338, 350, pl. 25.

Plate XXXIX a

The Mother of God Blessing Luke and the Painting of Icons.
Greek, sixteenth-seventeenth century. 31.6 × 49.3 × 2.5 cm.
Sinai, Monastery of St. Catherine. Catholicon, south aisle.
Lit.: Unpublished.

Plate XXXIX b

Sunday of Orthodoxy 'The Restoration of the Icons'.
Greek (Asia Minor), 1725. 40.5 × 29 × 2 cm.
Switzerland, Zumikon. Collection Ing. Hans Bibus.
Lit.: M. Chatzidakis, et al., *Les icones dans les collections suisses*, Berne 1968, no. 119.

Plate XL a

Saints Adoring an Icon with the Presentation of Virgin into the Temple.
Russian (Moscow), eighteenth century. 32 × 27.5 × 9 cm.
Switzerland, Kölliken. Collection Dr. S. Amberg-Herzog, no. 121.
Lit.: M. Chatzidakis, et al., *Les icones dans les collections suisses*, Berne 1968, no. 185.

Plate XL b

The Sleep of the Just.
Russian, eighteenth century. 31 × 25 × 2.5 cm.
Switzerland, Kölliken. Collection Cr. S. Amberg-Herzog, no. 163.
Lit.: M. Chatzidakis, et al., *Les icones dans les collections suisses*, Berne 1968, no. 181.

Plate XLI a

Battle between Novgorodians and Suzdalians and the Miracle of the Icon of the Virgin of the Sign.
Russian (Novgorod), last quarter of fifteenth century. 133 × 90 cm.
Moscow, Tretyakov Gallery, inv. no. 14454, cat. no. 103.
In the top register the icon of Mary is carried out of the Church of the Saviour at Novgorod where it was kept, and it is taken to the Kremlin. There it is met by adoring faithful. In the second register Novgorodian warriors stand on the town-fortress with the icon beside them while their fellows ride to meet the Suzdalians. In the third register one sees the battle and the defeat of the Suzdalians who struck the icon.
Lit.: K. Onasch, *Icons*, London 1961, no. 43.

Plate XLI b

The Discovery and Elevation of the True Cross, Constantine and Helena and the Decapitation of John the Baptist by the hierodeacon Joachim, (left wing of a triptych closed, detail).
Greek, second half sixteenth century. Left wing 25 × 17.5 cm.
U.S.A., Houston, Texas. The Museum of Fine Arts, Huston, gift of Miss Annette Finnigan.
Lit.: Unpublished.
Photo, Museum, photographer A. Mewbourn, Houston.

Plate XLII a

The Relic of St. Spyridon with Nicholas of Myra and Charalampes.
Greek (Ionian islands), eighteenth century. 38 × 30 × 2 cm.
Toronto, The Royal Ontario Museum, cat. no. U. 12.
Lit.: Unpublished.

Plate XLII b

St. Catherine and Mount Sinai.
Greek, seventeenth century. 31.8 × 218 cm.
Munich, Stadtmuseum, Stiftung Prof. Marchioni, inv. no. 69/962.
On the left is the Moses-peack, where Moses received the Law, on the right is the peak

of St. Catherine where angels deposited her body and at the foot of the mountain is the monastery of St. Catherine.

Lit.: *Ikonen*, Exhibition Catalogue, Haus der Kunst München, Munich 1970, no. 86.

Plate XLIII

Panorama of Mount Sinai with its Holy Sites.

Greek, sixteenth century. Painted on canvas 75.5 × 114.4 cm.

Formerly Geneva, Musée d'art et d'histoire, inv. no. M.A.H., M.F./3834. The icon was destroyed by fire on May 17, 1973.

Lit.: G. Galavaris, "A Bread Stamp from Sinai and Its Relatives," *Jahrbuch der österreichischen Byzantinistik*, 27(1978), 329-342.

Plate XLIV

Topography of the Holy Land.

Palestine, about 1800. Painted on canvas, 44 × 48.5 cm.

Switzerland, Richenthal. Collection Curée J. K. Felber, Pfarrei St. Cäcilia, no. 50.

It is painted on canvas so that it could be rolled and carried easier by pilgrims. In the middle of the composition is the Holy Sepulchre and related to it are Passion scenes; on the upper left, the Lake of Genesareth, in the middle Christ's Baptism and to the right the Dead Sea. Below, on the left, the monastery of St. John and below Judas hanging himself; on the opposite side above, Bethlehem and below an icon of St. Demetrius; other scenes and personages from the Old Testament including two of the evangelists' symbols, the angel and the calf.

Lit.: M. Chatzidakis, et al., *Les icones dans les collections suisses*, Berne 1968, no. 112.

Plate XLV

Mother of God "Source of Life" with the Emperor Leopold I and his Wife Eleonora Magdalena with Great Feasts, Apostles and Saints.

Greek (Mount Athos), about 1676-1705. 94 × 74.7 × 2.4 cm.

Vienna, Kunsthistorisches Museum, Gemäldegalerie, inv. no. 7000.

Lit.: K. Kreidl-Papadopoulos, "Die Ikonen im Kunsthistorischen Museum in Wien," *Jahrbuch der Kunsthistorischen Sammlungen in Wien*, 66 (1970), no. 16, fig. 55.

Plate XLVI a

Mother of God "Source of Life".

Greek, eighteenth century. 60 × 44 cm.

Aachen, Suermondt Museum, no. 20 in 1932 Museum's catalogue. Icon destroyed in the second world war.

A water spring in Constantinople, associated with the Mother of God, became a pilgrims' site. At the fall of Constantinople a miracle was reported. A monk saw the fish which he had fried jump living, out of the pan, in the spring and thus he believed that the great city had fallen into the hands of the Turks.

The icon represents the pilgrimages and the fish of the legend.

Lit.: F. Muthmann, *Mutter und Quelle*, Basel 1975, pl. 36.1.

Photo, Ann Gold, Kasino Str. 21, Aachen.

Plate XLVI b

The Virgin of Vladimir and the Family Tree of Moscow's Rulers by Simon Ushakov.
Russian (Moscow), 1668. 105 × 62 cm.
Moscow, Tretyakov Gallery, inv. no. 28598, cat. no. 912.
The medallions contain the princes of the court and of the Russian Church. The tree is
planted by the Metropolitan Peter and the Great Prince Ivan Danilovitch. The members
of the new dynasty of Tzars are around the tree. Above Christ spreads His protective
mantle.
Lit.: K. Onasch, *Icons*, London 1961, no. 133.

Plate XLVI c

Mother of God, John the Alms-Giver and Donors.
Cyprus, sixteenth century. 70 × 92 cm.
Formerly in the monastery of St. John Chrysostom, Cyprus.
The icon has been lost since the Turkish invasion.
Lit.: A. Papageorgiou, *Ikonen aus Zypern*, Munich-Geneva-Paris 1969, pl. on p. 104.
Photo, Dept. of Antiquities Nicosia, Cyprus.

Plate XLVII a

Mother of God "Hodegetria" and Donors.
Cyprus, 1529. 150 × 94.5 cm.
Cyprus, Church of St. Cassianos, Nicosia.
The Mother of God with half figures of two angels above her and three seraps behind her.
Below there is a three-aisled basilica with a bell tower and Gothic windows held by two
angels. On the northern side in the centre is an icon of the Virgin Eleousa below which an
inscription gives the names of donors and the date. The donors are kneeling and praying
on either side of the icon.
Lit.: A. Papageorgiou, *Byzantine Icons of Cyprus*, Benaki Museum, Exhibition Catalogue
Athens 1976, no. 36.

Plate XLVII b

The Coronation of the Virgin (Left wing from a triptych).
Crusader icon, thirteenth century. 56.8 × 47.5 × 5 cm.
Sinai, Monastery of St. Catherine. Old Library, south wall.
Lit.: K. Weitzmann "Icon Painting in the Crusader Kingdom," *Dumbarton Oaks Papers*,
20 (1966), 59 fig. 16.

Plate XLVIII

"The Prophets from Above" by Stamatios Thytes.
Greek, 1610-1628. 92 × 66.5 × 2.5 cm.
Patmos, Church Hagia ton Hagion. Chapel of the Holy Ghost.
Lit.: M. Chatzidakis, *Eikones tes Patmou*, Athens 1977, no. 113, pl. 163.
Photo, National Bank of Greece, courtesy of the Monastery of St. John, Patmos.

PLATES I-XLVIII

c. Moscow, Christ by Rublyov

b. Stockholm, Christ Pantocrator

a. Sinai, Christ Pantocrator

a. Sinai, King Abgarus (detail)

c. Richenthal, Switzerland, The Holy Face

b. Moscow, The Holy Face by Pervusha

Plate IV   *The Holy Trinity*

a. Athens, The Hospitality of Abraham

b. London, Paternity

c. Private Coll. The Trinity

b. Athens, "Galactotrophousa"

a. Palermo, "Hodegetria"

c. Moscow, The Virgin of Don by Theophanes

a. Princeton, The Virgin of the "Passion"

c. Echteld, The Virgin of the Sign

b. Venice, "Blachernitissa"

b. Cleveland, The Virgin Enthroned

a. Freising, The Virgin Orans

Plate VIII　　　　　　　　*The Old Testament*

Athens, Abraham's Sacrifice

a. Sinai, The Three Children

b. San Diego, Calif., The Three Children

c. Athens, Daniel

Plate X *The Old Testament*

a. Sinai, Elijah

c. Athens, Elijah's Ascension

b. Echteld, Elijah's Ascension

Madison, Deesis and Dodekaorton

Plate XII   *The Incarnation—The Great Feasts*

b. Moscow, Annunciation   c. Sinai, Annunciation

a. Sinai, The Twelve Feasts

b. Echteld, Annunciation

a. Sinai, Annunciation

Plate XIV   *The Incarnation—The Great Feasts*

Sinai, Birth and Infancy of Christ

a. Jerusalem, The Baptism   b. Belgrade, The Baptism

c. Oxford, The Raising of Lazarus

a. Athens, The Crucifixion

c. Athens, The Descent from the Cross

b. Athens, The Crucifixion by Pavias

b. Athos, the "Chairete"

a. Hann Coll., The Marys at the Sepulchre

Plate XVIII   *The Incarnation— The Great Feasts*

Venice, The Descent into Hell

a. Berlin, The Descent into Hell

b. Echteld, The Ascension

c. Athos, Pentecost

Plate XX   *The Incarnation—The Great Feasts*

a. Moscow, The Dormition by Theophanes
the Greek

c. Echteld, The Dormition

b. Vienna, The Dormition

a. Cyprus, Gabriel

c. Jerusalem, The Miracle at Chonai

b. Sinai, Michael and Donor

d. Kölliken, Michael Conquers Satan

Plate XXII   *The Church, Apostles-Saints*

a. Holland, Private Coll. John the Baptist

b. Athos, Peter by Euphrosynos

c. Cyprus, Paul

a. Patmos, Meeting Peter and Paul

b. Athos, Peter and Paul   c. Aachen, Nicholas of Myra

Plate XXIV　　　　　*The Church, Apostles-Saints*

Athens, John Chrysostom "Fountain of Wisdom"

a. Belgrade, Demetrius

b. Athens, George

c. Hann Coll., George

d. Private Coll., George

Plate XXVI   *The Church, Saints*

a. Sinai, Saints September-November   b. San Diego, Calif., The Forty Martyrs of Sebaste

c. Toronto, Martyrdom of St. Charalampes

a. Athens, Christopher the Cynocephalos   b. Ottawa, Christ with Saints

c. Echteld, Nicholas of Mozajsk

Plate XXVIII

a. Paris, Christ with Abt Menas

b. Belgrade, Sts Sava and Simeon

c. Amsterdam, Sts Sabas and Euthymius

b. Kölliken, Simeon Stylite the Elder

c. Madison, Basil the Great and Basil the Blessed

a. Zumikon, Onuphrios

a. Sinai, The Heavenly Ladder

b. Jerusalem, The Death of Ephraim the Syrian by Pavias

Sinai, Transfiguration and the Raithou Martyrs by Klonza

Plate XXXII　　　　　　　　　　*Liturgy-Worship*

Moscow, Iconostasis, Royal Doors

a. Venice, Great Deesis

b. Moscow, The Holy Face

c. Moscow, The Adoration of the Cross

a. Patmos, The Lamentation

b. Athens, Christ the "Vine"

c. Recklinghausen, Christ the "Vine"

a. Rome, Christ "Image of Pity"

b. Sinai, Christ "King of Glory"

c. Rhode Island, Mary of Egypt

Plate XXXVI   *Liturgy-Worship*

Toronto, The Divine Liturgy

a. Athens, Confession

b. Vienna, Confession

Plate XXXVIII   *Theology and Life*

b. Recklinghausen, Siren

c. Athens, Eros by Deutereuon Siphnou

a. Vienna, The Glorification of the Soul

a. Sinai, Mary Blessing Luke and the Icons

b. Zumikon, The Triumph of the Icons

b. Kölliken, The Sleep of the Just

a. Kölliken, Saints Adoring an Icon

b. Houston, Texas, The Discovery of the True Cross

a. Moscow, A Miracle of the Icon of the Virgin of the Sign

Plate XLII　　　　　*The Cult of Relics, Loca Sancta*

b. Munich, St. Catherine

a. Toronto, The Relic of St. Spyridon

Geneva, The Holy Sites on Mt Sinai

Richenthal, The Holy Land

Vienna, Mother of God "Source of Life" and the Austrian Rulers

a. Aachen, Mother of God "Source of Life"

b. Moscow, The Family Tree of
Moscow's Rulers

c. Cyprus, Mother of God and Donors

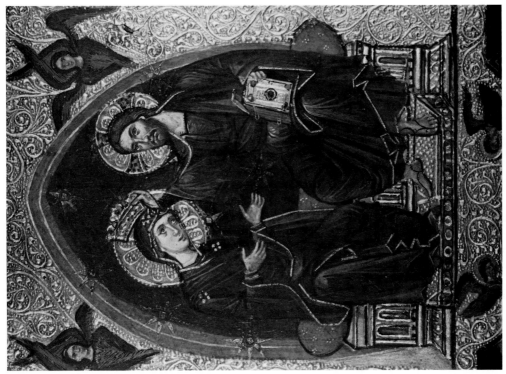

b. Sinai, The Coronation of the Virgin

a. Cyprus, Mother of God and Donors

Plate XLVIII   *Mariolatry*

Patmos, "The Prophets from Above"